Archetypes of Astrology

Unlocking the Mysteries of the
Planets, Signs & Houses

Ena Stanley

ACS Publications

Archetypes of Astrology
Unlocking the Mysteries of the Planets, Signs & Houses

by Ena Stanley

Cover and book design by Maria Kay Simms

Library of Congress Control Number 2012907554

International Standard Book Number: 978-1-934976-32-6

Published by ACS Publications, an imprint of Starcrafts LLC
334-A Calef Highway, Epping, NH 03042
http://www.starcraftspublishing.com
http://www.astrocom.com
http://www.acspublications.com

Printed in the United States of America

CONTENTS

Acknowledgements

The true author of this book is the essence of astrology; I only wanted it to make sense. As I state in Chapter 2, I stared and stared, while trying to understand—to completely grasp—each energy. I read books and mythology, listened to those who "knew," and came up with the seed of this work. The person who started me on the road to understanding, however, was the woman I consider my true mentor, Zipporah Dobyns, PhD. I can't imagine I would have had anything comprehensible without her teachings.

On the other hand, there is possibly not a teacher who can't say that what they teach they learned from their students. It was fifteen years of students' questions and reflections that rooted this seed firmly—starting with insights into the Scorpio Archetype and finally grasping, after intense struggle, the Gemini Archetype (my more prominent archetypal energy and subsequently the most difficult).

At that point in time, only the roots had taken hold. The plant was formed with the hard work and insights of Cheryl Whisman, Online College of Astrology's first Education Director, who quickly became my right hand. The plant flowered when Evan Bortnick joined forces and dabbed colors of brilliance into the work

To all above, I give my deep love and appreciation. I'm so glad you all were born!

Dedication
to

Eric Stanley
for
his support for
two decades

Chapter *1*

Antiquities, Astrology, Archetypes, Cabbages & Kings

Carl Jung's work inadvertently took the historic shackles off of astrology. Most immediately obvious is the revival and exaltation of mythology. Looking at mythology with a new respect has brought a deeper understanding, and consequently a deeper interpretation to Mercury, Venus, Jupiter, Pluto, and the rest of the planets. To really grasp the significance of archetypal astrology, however, this focuses on the bigger picture that is emerging out of current explorations.

As we enter the new millennium, it is becoming increasingly evident that the prediction of Bob Dylan's '60's song *"the times, they are a changin"* continues to roll out in front of us. It makes little difference how tightly one chooses to hold onto the reality of the "good old days," everyone is either drowning in, or swimming in, the dawning of a new age.

Dr. Jung's revolutionary work with mythology, psychic exploration, and subsequently his view of the archetypes and psychological development is only a small tributary to this expanding pool of transformation. Within Jung's synchronous collective unconscious paradigm, we are being inundated with data. And, of course, the invention of computers was a necessary vehicle to facilitate this unprecedented renaissance—for computers hold the massive amount of incoming data, correlate it, and then disperse it around the world at an unimaginable rate of speed. Furthermore, the data that is being held, correlated, and dispersed is coming in from every known area of intelligentsia: astrology, astronomy, archaeology, geology, medical-biology, psychology.

Subsequently, history is being re-viewed, revised, and rewritten, and no matter how wide or narrow one follows this new information, one thing is becoming increasingly evident: we cannot measure humanity's evolution by a linear struggle into ever increasing civilization. What originally appeared to be a straight line is currently taking the shape of a great circle. In addition, as the accumulated evidence is making the circle apparent, it is becoming even more apparent that the sequential progress was a series of "throwing babies out with the bathwater."

While every facet of history that comes into our consideration is totally fascinating, these writings are limited to the survey portion of the Western credo that reflects its opinion on femininity. Then by deduction, it is hoped that this treatise will present evidence of how this piece of history affected astrology. Without further hesitation, let's go right to the point by referring to a lecture given at the Cycles & Symbols Conference in San Francisco in 1990 by Dr. Richard Tarnas. Dr. Tarnas pointed out that the major figures who influenced our Western World view, *"from the very beginning until just day-before-yesterday,"* all had one very important thing in common – they were all men!

How much better could it be said? For the past three thousand years—give or take—we (as in the Western world) have been living within a masculine matrix.

Moreover, the recognition of any previously dominant matriarchal societies was lost some place in oblivion. This is not difficult to conceive if it is recognized that a social order is shaped by its myth of creation. The early beginnings of male dominance are clearly demonstrated within the Judeo-Christian myth of Adam and Eve.

At the onset, the creation of Eve—the feminine heroine in our myth—was for no other purpose than to be that of a helping hand. Her creation was more an after-thought than that of a deliberate act, and she came from a superfluous part of Adam, the Hero of our myth. On the other hand, one might find it curious that, within the two to four thousand years that this myth has been the core provocation of Western belief, no one ever noticed that lions, tigers, lizards, fishes, and birds possessed both males and females in their respective species, even though their creation was reportedly before humans. In addition, none of the other males in these species had to give up a rib!

It's also interesting to consider a myth that is said to have preceded this one—the myth of Lilith. To impart a long and fascinating story in a rather brief fashion, Lilith and Adam were created together, out of the same clay. When it came time for them to couple, however, there ensued an argument about who was going to be on top. When Lilith realized that neither of them was going to give an inch, she left the garden.

It's interesting to note that she wasn't driven out, nor did she drive Adam out, she simply left. Adam then called upon God, who set up a new arrangement by extracting the infamous rib, thereby creating Adam's second attempt at coupling out of his own body, and making the 'pecking order' clearer. The symbolism here is quite clear: only by a process of mutual consent can one side of a polarity be degraded and treated unjustly. The feminine is simply much too powerful to accept such degradation without a degree of consent. This too, inevitably, has its purpose— substantiated by a commentary made by Dr. Jung on the *Secret of the Golden Flower,* when he said he had learned that the most important problems of life are basically insoluble, and because of that, they simply must be outgrown.

Women, however, were not the only creatures within the myth of Adam and Eve who were treated unjustly: how many of you are repulsed at the very mention of the word snake? What do you do when you think you've seen one? In reality, the snake is no more than a very shy creature, one who plays an important role in the eco-system. Moreover, only a sparse number of snakes, in a species count of literally hundreds, could possibly harm a human.

Nevertheless, the snake's archetypal crime is to be the symbol of cyclic death and rebirth within the feminine paradigm. By its nature, the snake sets a cyclic pattern: when the snake takes in food, it must go through the process of shedding its old skin and growing a new one. The synthesis of the food into its body, food that will facilitate its growth, renders the snake blind and vulnerable. Absolutely metaphoric!

Coupled with the above metaphor, like a hand and glove, is the ingestion of the fruit from the tree. Any student of modern occultism has a predisposition about the symbolism of a tree. To digest fruit from the tree of knowledge...I believe the word for that is wisdom!

The very core of the patriarchal myth defiles and devalues every sacred symbolism within the feminine paradigm. Therefore, to assure that a patriarchal matrix had its fair quotient of human history, it was man's competitive obligation to destroy woman. What better way to stage total alienation than to make one totally accountable for all of humanity's wrong-doing? From this platform of "evil," woman and her ancestral symbols were exiled. Therefore, the "Order of Buck-Passing" became our culture's credo: "It ain't me, Lord! It was this woman, here!" This, of course, gave woman full responsibility for her own rape—literally and figuratively.

Subsequently, women have been discounted, disregarded, and even feared for most of their innate feminine wisdoms. Woman's beauty was converted into temptation, her sensuality was shameful, and her life-giving miracle—childbirth—became a punishment to be suffered.

What has been delineated above just didn't begin at dawn one day, nor had it always been the prevailing social norm. All known cultures processed through some degree of a matriarchal matrix. With the vigilance of first the Jews, then the Christians, and lastly the Muslims, the total patriarchal conversion gradually progressed until eventually, like the Moon at total eclipse, the patriarchal paradigm overwhelmed the matriarchy causing it to fade into the darkness. The darkness of this feminine moon was obviously present throughout the past one thousand years, but it reached its apex over the past three to five hundred years. The evidence of this apex is the patriarchal God named Reason, and the assertion of Western ideology onto every culture on the planet.

Nonetheless, the feminine paradigm of Earth is again aligning with the Sun and Moon, and that gnawing, stirring, primordial wisdom of the lost matriarch is emerging back into the light of awareness. The pervasion of the feminine is confirming its unequivocal importance in the new dawn's light. To clearly see where this is going, however, and ultimately to see the premise that is emerging as modern astrology, it is necessary to define the primary differences between the matriarchal and patriarchal matrix.

The major distinction within the patriarchal matrix is the decisive separateness between the individual psyche and the natural world. This is amply reflected within the patriarchal myth by the fact that man places his god outside himself. Moreover, he even sees himself alienated from his god. He has given himself hope, however: man is redemptive to his god because of the presence of the consciousness or soul. (Only within the past hundred years or so has it been common thought that woman has a soul, as well as man, and therefore also has hope of absolute redemption!)

On the other hand, in the general thinking of many, the world, or environment, has no hope of redemption. The world (lakes, rocks, trees, animals, planets, etc.) lacks consciousness or soul. Therefore, the hierarchy goes like this: nature—subservient by alienation to man; and man—subservient by alienation to God. By supremacy, God controls man; and within the hierarchical structure, it's man's right to control and/or conquer the natural (and/or instinctual) world. Basically, God kicks man; man kicks dog.

Within the patriarchal matrix, it is man's inalienable right and duty to bring the world into submission—through might, and consequently through reason. (If something needs to be conquered, and the thing that is to be conquered is mightier than the conqueror, then the conqueror must reason out how to conquer it.) Consequently, from this position, man controls through judgments—what is good and what is bad, what is right and what is wrong. There is a distinct duality within this matrix.

Antithetically, the matriarchal reality implies a type of unity. The universe is one, congruent whole. This reality sees everything connected to everything else, and everything affected, in turn, affects humanity. The supreme consciousness (or God/Goddess) lives within all things, and as well, all things reside within the God/Goddess. Separation was uncommon within this reality matrix. Consequently, everything in the world has equality—along with the self.

In his lecture at the 1990 Cycles & Symbols Conference, Dr. Richard Tarnas described the matriarchal reality most adequately when he said that it sees a natural world...one that is saturated with a psychologically different meaning...a world that is permeated with spiritual beings that can communicate with us, giving us purpose. *"Things resonate with spiritual and psychological significance. The world is animated with the same psychological realities that we experience within ourselves."* He concluded by saying that the *"world is in soul..."* and we interact and participate in this world.

Dr. Jung's theory of the collective unconscious adds credence to the matriarchal matrix. In both—Tarnas' description of the matriarchal reality and Jung's collective unconscious— everything speaks of everything else, and therefore, everything has a symbolic, as well as a literal meaning. Within this paradigm, a planet's reflection is in a myth; a myth is reflected in psychological development; and the movement of a planet can be traced in a human's progression. There is no beginning or ending, no separation, no restrictive judgments of idiosyncrasies within the world of experience.

It is also important to become clear about what is specifically meant when the word patriarchy is used. It does not necessarily mean man. Nor, does matriarchy mean woman. In other words, a woman can administrate a patriarchal society; one example would be Queen Elizabeth I. Subsequently, many societies that fit within the matriarchal matrix were supervised by men, i.e., many of the Native American cultures. My point is that both patriarchal and matriarchal matrices are ideologies. The patriarchal ideal is to put reality into a structure, a tangible, conceivable order—to ultimately see reason behind the chaos and virtually alter or predict humanity's fate. On the other side, the matriarchal ideal is to recognize that all things have dignity and purpose—to be quiet and to listen to what is being said. Both have value; both have something important to contribute.

Anyone knows that if you go in one direction long enough, far enough, you'll come back to your starting position. The same applies to ideologies; only arrogance assumes that one direction is superior to another. To again sway totally to a matriarchal matrix, diminishing the value of the patriarchal matrix, is just throwing another baby out with the bathwater. The present conversion dictates a cynosure—that which can direct or guide—to incorporate both matrices into a workable, comprehensible paradigm.

Interestingly enough, just by its nature, the comprehension of astrology embraces both the matriarchal and patriarchal matrices. The wise ones searched for understanding in the cosmos so that they could control the environment. This originated from the skeletal structure of the patriarchal matrix. This line of thinking eventually led to the innovation of mathematics and physics.

On the other hand, astrology was begotten in the matriarchal matrix. It encompasses the phenomenon that the physical world has an intelligent language that readily communicates meaning. (This rudimentary fact has been its only crime and incited its alienation during the patriarchal eclipse.) Consequently, astrology is an existing cynosure of both matrices: it definitely has structure that can stand up to scientific studies with honor and correctness, (similar to any psychological evaluations). Astrology tells a story of the instinctual, psychic development of the consciousness within the language of the cosmos.

Carl Jung presented an astrological Rosetta stone, and we can now expand the knowledge within the language of the cosmos. He brought a new, dignified way of extracting meaning through his archetypal paradigm.

Archetypal energy is universal within all human development, whether one is a bush-man in the tropics of Africa or an English nobleman. The development of human consciousness (ego) is through a myriad of unconscious directives; however, each of these directives is contained neatly in twelve divisions of basic human development. For example, each individual has an archetypal image of Mother. This image prevails in spite of what an individual's mother is like. As well, one struggles with the internal needs for individuality and the claim for personal space, on the one hand, while on the other, one adjusts to the demands of their particular social rules.

Astrology leaves no part of human development dangling. Nothing within basic human development is unexplained. Moreover, the astrological paradigm takes randomness out of archetypal observance and puts it into a succinct order. Together they elevate one's perception to a level beyond that of normal chaotic living, beyond random occurrences and events, and hurl conscious development into a purposeful sequence.

The material in this book will reflect these archetypal stages of human development in the astrological paradigm; as well, it will show that a series of archetypes are the main constituent of astrology. It is my purpose in this treatise to show that it is impossible to separate one from the other. For example, is the fact that the planet Venus dazzles in our sky because she is veiled with dense, noxious gases nothing more than a random coincidence to her provocative counterpart in mythology? Or is this just additional evidence of a collective unconscious, where all things truly exist side by side, and by synchronicity tell the existence of the other.

Chapter 2

Introduction to Archetypes

When I began studying astrology formally (i.e., in a classroom), my instructor stood in the front of the room and read lists of keywords for the signs, then for the planets, then finally those for the houses. We were to memorize these keywords, and, from that point, to learn to read a chart.

I was not an astrological novice when I entered her class; I had studied astrology on my own for eleven years. Consequently, I had become personally familiar with some of the words she used, especially the words pertaining to Saturn! Most of the words she used, however, went together in my head and fell into an enigmatic pit. Often the same words were repeated within totally different jurisdictions, and that confused me, even though, in retrospect, the same word could, in fact, fit into both paradigms.

Nonetheless, it took many years of reflection before a keyword had much depth.

At the end of two years of formal study, I had absorbed much of value from my first instructor, and to some degree, I had even learned the preparatory process necessary for delineation; but I was completely ignorant when it came to understanding what it all truly meant.

Aside and along with astrology, I had been a student of Behavioral and Gestalt Psychology. When I decided to become a professional astrologer, it was my ambition to utilize astrology as a psychological counseling tool. Within my independent study, I had already experienced that an astrological chart could take me into deeper insights than other methods—into a soulful understanding. Now, even though keywords are an invaluable means of dealing with astrological fundamentals, at the onset, forming sentences with a string of cookbook keywords lacked depth and didn't feel very soulful to me! After I had completed those two years of study, I instantly realized that my education had just begun.

Long before I got a personal understanding of "manifesting what you want," I'd heard of Dr. Zipporah Dobyns, the clinical psychologist who had merged astrology and psychology, so my only focus for a year or so became to study with her. It wasn't long until I manifested that connection. Her method was everything and more than I'd dreamed it to be. Her 12-Letter Alphabet was the actual doorknob that would open a door so I could get a different grasp of understanding. With my original orientation of fundamental astrological learning (modern), and Zip's unique paradigm, it was only a slight step into Jungian psychology and archetypes. One could safely say that Zip's 12-Letter Alphabet is the rudimentary concept of an archetype.

At this point, I want to do a little side-step and jump right into an explanation of archetypes; but even more important, I want to establish what the word archetype means to me—what it means when I say archetype. Once this meaning is clear, everything else will fall neatly into its proper place.

The word archetype comes from the Platonic era of the rational mind and critical rationalism. Originally it was synonymous with prototype, and it got its contemporary meaning in depth psychology from Carl Gustav Jung.

To summarize Dr. Jung's brilliant work, we must start with Sigmund Freud. With Carl Jung as his student, Freud determined that the conscious mind (ego) was predestined by the unconscious mind (id). From that basic premise, Jung began to extrapolate and, in time, varied from Freud. To greatly simplify, Jung discovered that all peoples, in spite of their culture, had homologous instinctual directives initiating conscious development. One of his major breakthroughs came when he intensely studied the myths and folklore of totally different cultures and found consistent similarities

Dr. Jung also noticed yet another phenomenon. He observed that there were incalculable numbers of circumstances where two seemingly unrelated situations would aptly coincide with each other. We know these situations by the name coincidence. An example would be telling a story and simultaneously having a specific part of that story physically appear. Jung concluded that there was a definite order and meaning to what appeared as random circumstance. That order, he theorized, was a collective unconscious—a cosmic holding tank where all things are contemporaneous and exist side by side. Within the collective unconscious, there is no linear time, no sequence of events. From this position, he found the development of the individual was symmetrically reflected in the stages of the history of humanity as told through mythology. It became evident that individuals carried certain structural elements and these revealed themselves to the conscious mind through instinctual pictorial images such as fantasies and dreams. These images instigate the process of conscious reactions and assimilations. He named those structural elements of the collective unconscious archetypes.

It is within this Jungian paradigm that I use the word archetype.

Returning to Zip Dobyns and her 12-Letter Alphabet, the value of the alphabet concept is straightforward. Zip's brilliance saw the thread that wove together a very basic astrological premise. Instead of coercing the mind to stitch twelve separate signs to twelve unshared houses, along with ten different planets, struggling to get the paradox into cohesive comprehension, Zip's 12-Letter Alphabet simply melted away the dilemma. She merely affiliated the sign with its house and ruling planet, making each of them mutual. As Zip says, *"It's as if you have the letter 'P'*

—it doesn't matter if the P is a capital P, a small p, a cursive p, or a fancy P, they are all the letter P, and you interpret them as such." From that premise, one can look at the 8th house, Scorpio, or Pluto and call a predominance of any one of them an emphasis on "Letter 8." Then, a psychological theme emerges.

So, within the 12-Letter Alphabet model, one would take Aries, the First House, and Mars as equal representatives of the Letter 1; Taurus, the Second House and Venus would subsequently represent Letter 2; and so forth.

As one goes deeper into the profundity of astrology, however, it becomes evident that the assumption of the 12-Letter Alphabet is indeed too casual. Nonetheless, for a preliminary concept, it introduces an image that, to me, outdoes many others. A beginning student or anyone new to astrology can more easily comprehend the similarity of theme components when they are defined, as Zip did, into the "12 Letters."

Moreover, due to the genesis of my own personal learning experience—going from enigmatic confusion with chart delineation into the snug concentration of the 12-Letter Alphabet—I see myself as having blossomed from the above. In other words, I did not experience Zip's system as faulty as many astrologers do, but rather I saw it as a womb that gave me the birth of my conceptual astrology.

That birth has been the recapitulation of the nuances between the signs and houses and planets. Instead of a new befuddlement, however, the nuances emerged uniformly into an archetypal paradigm. Parallel to each astrological archetype, made up of sign, houses and planet, each Jungian archetype has a distinct orientation that shows itself through diverse faces. Within the Mother Archetype, for instance, there is the Great Mother, the Nurturing Mother, the Terrible Mother, the Benevolent Mother, the Jealous Mother, the Wicked Mother—the images go on and on.

Now, even though there are definable and distinct components, I tend to think of the three components—signs/houses/planets —in the same manner as one sees maternal triplets: the more familiar one is with the three distinct personalities, the more conspicuous their differences are. And, of course, to the newly acquainted, or to the passerby, the triplets may look identical.

Moreover, there is a certain hierarchy among these three astrological components. Continuing with the "triplet" metaphor, a planet is like the first-born: strong, outstanding, vital, intense—the leader of the three. The house is the second-born: orienting, grounding, establishing, familiarizing—the consistent, unchanging triplet. The triplet born last is the representative of the sign. This is the triplet that often seems a bit weaker at birth; but then there seems to be a burst of energy that can spring up from some unknown source. This triplet is integrating, blending, amiable, compliant—the socialite of the three, empathetic and outgoing.

To extrapolate, the planet is the "thing" with which we are dealing. It physically sits out there in space, and has size and form, and that physical size and form is equally metaphoric. Each planet has a unique and distinguishable character that becomes outstanding within the planet/house/sign affiliation. (It should be noted that Sun and Moon, although technically not planets, are commonly included when astrologers speak of "planets" in general. Sometimes, in books and articles, the term "Lights" is used to distinguish Sun and Moon from Mercury, Venus, Mars, etc.. When I refer to planets as a general group here, I am including Sun and Moon.)

The other two of our three astrological components, the signs and houses, are a bit more intangible than the planets. They are not actually things one can look at within our physical reality, but they are very important in understanding how to read a chart.

The signs are 12 equal divisions of the 360° circle, 30° for each sign. While they were orignally named for the constellations long ago, due to the precession of the equinoxes, the constellations and the signs of astrology do not sync nearly as well with each other as they once did. Nevertheless, the archetypal symbolism of astrological signs still work well in astrological interpretation.

The houses of a chart wheel (or horoscope) are twelve

mathematical divisions of the circle that are derived from time and location of birth. Although some choose to use equal houses, most astrologers use the unequal houses that result from the date-time-location calculations. Primary in forming the houses of a horoscope are the vertical and horizontal cross that divides the circle into four sections. and define what astrologers call the **angles** of the chart. The points on the wheel where the vertical line of the cross begins and ends are called the Midheaven (MC) at the top, or South/Day of the chart wheel, and the Imum Coeli (IC) at the bottom, or North/Night of the chart wheel). The end points of the horizontal line that intersects the vertical are called the Ascendant (ASC) at the left or east-rising point, and the Descendant (DSC) at the right or west-setting point of the circle.

The chart wheel is further segmented with lines that form three houses between each of the angles, for a total of twelve houses that are numbered counter-clockwise from the Ascendant, 1 though 12. On the next page, for the benefit of those readers who may be new to astrology, is an illustration of a basic chart wheel showing the house divisions and angles.

The angles of a chart are more tangible than the signs, because they are based on exact time and location of birth, so they are next in hierarchy after the planets. The houses, subdivisions of the angles, are grounded in as much as the houses are actually a division of space surrounding the earth, specifically anchored to one's locality. From this fixed position, we see the Sun, Moon and planets move through the degrees of the zodiac signs, rise and set, culminate and anti-culminate.

As is apparent with the study of the chart's hemispheres, this creates a particular mood that corresponds to the time of the day. The result is that the angles are fixed, constant, and are metaphorical of light/dark, internal/external, subjective/objective correlations. As you will witness, these twelve divisions will continue to enhance and define the arrangement and moods of the hemispheres, and subsequently, of the quadrants.

To reflect upon the signs of the Zodiac, I will go to the ancients. The 1990's brought many translations of astrology's

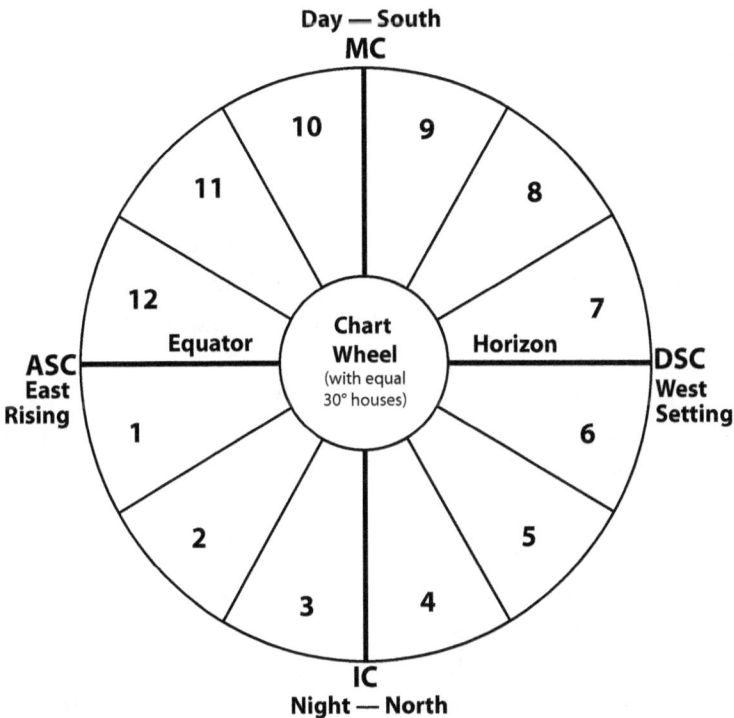

Day — South
MC

10   9
11   8
12   7
ASC East Rising — Equator — Chart Wheel (with equal 30° houses) — Horizon — DSC West Setting
1   6
2   5
3   4

IC
Night — North

ancient texts, one of which was the works of *Paulus Alexandrinus* translated by Robert Schmidt. The part that I am primarily interested in sharing with you concerns the signs. The signs are often thought of as minor arbitrary things superimposed behind the Ecliptic—either by the constellations, or by the equinoxes and solstices. When reading the publications that emerged from the Schmidt translations, I attained an even deeper meaning of the signs. We get our "signs" from the ancient Greek word *zōidion*, which, through modern translation, seems to have two basic meanings: a living thing and a picture or image.

Robert Schmidt says in a personal commentary within a footnote that *"...a living thing and a picture were both called a zoidia out of some analogy the Greeks saw in them..."* Within the text, he relates that Plato hinted at this analogy in the *Epinomis*, There he defined *zōidion* as an *"alliance of the soul and body that gives birth to a shape..."* It's the supposition that the stars themselves are gods, or, images the gods have created to represent themselves. Robert concluded by saying that *"the soul informs the body"* similar to a sculptor shaping his material.

What I gleaned from the above information is that the signs shape, or define, the planet's personality: "an alliance of soul and body that gives birth to a shape." Now, when we say, "I'm a Leo" or "I'm a Gemini" or "I'm a Pisces," we can see the very soul of the signs entering our bodies to sculpt us into animation. We can now look at the signs as imparting an activation of a particular disposition.

The signs have yet another significance. They connect the Tropical Zodiac to the Sidereal Zodiac, in as much as the names are the same in each system—the signs of the Tropical system kept the same names of their corresponding constellations in the Sidereal system. Within the traditional Tropical system, however, the signs relate to the seasons instead of the constellations. Every year, within a 24-hour or so period of time, the Sun, on its journey from the south to the north, crosses exactly on the earth's equator. With that particular position of the Sun (apparently traveling around the earth from our point of view), the earth experiences a day that exactly equals the night. That moment in time/space is called the Vernal Equinox, and begins our Zodiacal signs with Aries.

One more important thing: looking at the seasons, we would emerge with something that closely resembles Fire, Earth, Air, and Water, with Fire representing spring, Earth producing the fruits of summer, Air intellectualizing autumn, and the quietude of Water can definitely be winter. Each sign, house and planet is associated with one of the four elements.

Moreover, just in case you haven't noticed it already, the planets, houses, and signs also correspond closely to a Cardinal, Fixed and Mutable formulation. Cardinal signs are intiating and action oriented. Fixed signs express stability and a sustaining quality. Mutable signs are changeable.

Astrology has a rhythm that is played out in 3/4 time, and it is repeated over and over. Of the three signs of each element:

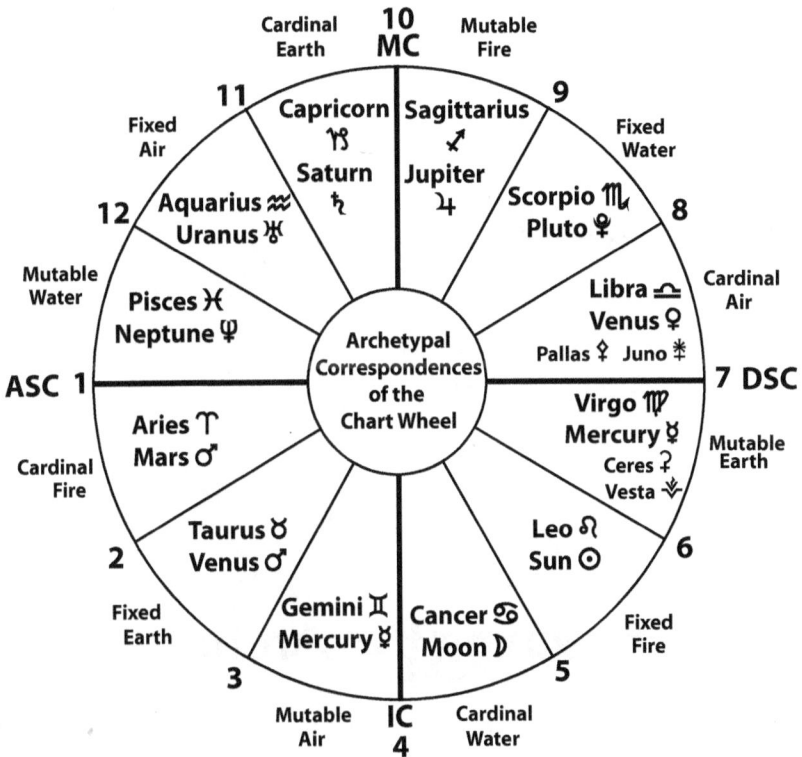

(fire, earth, air, water), the first is Cardinal, the second is Fixed and the third is Mutable. I have never found anything that didn't fit, in some way, into this pattern. The illustraton of a chart wheel above shows the "natural zodiac" and the element, mode, sign and planetary correspondences associated with each division of the wheel.

In fact, every archetypal correspondence we encounter in studying astrology—planet, sign, house, element, mode— fits snugly into the piece before, without cutting corners, or chopping off parts. After studying the subject for close to a half a century, I can give you this statement of truth: If you don't get an instant hit of consistency while studying a particular facet of astrology, keep staring. It'll come. Moreover, when you finally see the congruency, you will have also become more enlightened.

Chapter 3

Approaching the Archetypes

I want to say a few more words about a way to see the astrological language and how the diversity of that language is clearly classified into an archetypal axiom. Each distinctive archetypal energy has a myriad of ways of expressing itself, and throughout the astrological world, keywords have been used to pull those diversified images into view and group them together. Each planet, sign, or house has traditionally ruled certain events and/or objects throughout the ages. It is not my intention for this material to eliminate keywords—quite the contrary. Instead, I want my material to be experienced as a keyword shelf, on which each and every known as well as every yet-to-be-known keyword can comfortably rest. I want you, the student, to be able to see every object, situation, and behavior as a keyword and be able to glean its astrological association through the study of this material.

It is also valuable to think of keywords as key concepts or as key principles. Recalling the reference in the previous chapter to Schmidt's translation from Paulus Alexandrinus of the Greek word *Zōidion* as a living thing, a picture or image, you can get a good feeling for what is meant here. The Archetypes of which we're speaking are GODS! They are mega-large cosmic entities. They represent vital Cosmic Principles as well as dynamic Human Needs. Keep this in mind when considering keywords. Don't let this restrict your thinking to forms of manifestation. It's similar to the platonic idea realm through which form emerges. We're not referring here to descriptions of behavior; we're referring to Ontology—to numinous Being itself.

Remember those times when you have a sense of something profound moving behind the experienceable world. Conjure that sensation and find words to describe it when dealing with these keywords.

At the end of many of the chapters in this book, ponder the appropriate concepts that particular words represent. Imagine twelve great pillars holding up the entire universe and all that it contains. These pillars aren't material in substance—they are Ideas...Principles. Around these principles, our Solar System took its form. Imagine further that from each of these twelve Pillars, energy radiates outward in ever-widening circles, taking in and giving form and essence to ever more expressions.

Imagine these spiraling down through four basic levels. Naturally, the first level is the Cosmic Source itself—the Cosmic Principle. The next level is the hierarchy of Human Need structure. The third level is human attitudes, behavior, moods and personality characteristics, and the last level—the most mundane, so to speak—is things, happenings and occurrences.

What you inevitably notice when you move through these levels, from the Cosmic to the Mundane, is an increase in the number of descriptive words you can use for each. The Archetypes are quite fertile in this way; they increase through the levels of manifestation.

Examining each of the Archetypes from all of these levels will bring you into a richer and deeper plane of astrological comprehension. Astrology is often hamstringed by a description of mere effect or occurrence, and this disparity in comprehension makes a real difference when interacting with a client. Therefore, with this valuable thought-tool, you have the ability to give your listener a perspective that he/she, arguably, can obtain nowhere else—the perspective gained from astrology is unique.

Using the First Archetype for our example, let's ask ourselves, "What is the Cosmic Principle?" and after reading the material in the appropriate chapter, we might postulate that it is a quality of breakthrough, of strong beginning, perhaps even a quality of moving forward and outward. To put this into a single word, we might use assertion. When attempting to find words to describe the Source, it's best to try to come up with words that describe things that reach beyond the realm of human-ness— outside the realm of the biological—although our vocabulary for describing such concepts is somewhat limited.

Even the word assertion doesn't fully encapsulate the Cosmic Principle for the First Archetype. It does, however, express the idea of being-ness, of nothing holding it back— the sense of pure impulse, like a meteor surging forward through space. Assertion supports the image of an unstoppable forward-moving force—a force that breaks through, like a shoot pushing its way through dead leaves under the first rays of the spring sun, or a bird cracking open its egg to begin life.

In Abraham Maslow's book, *Toward a Psychology of Being*, he presented a theory of the hierarchy of human needs. He described these as "meta-needs," and they are hierarchical because they must be satisfied in order. This hierarchical need-structure, which was inspired by Dr. Maslow, was given astrological form by the respected astrologer/ psychologist, Dr. Glenn Perry, Ph.D. This then is what is being evoked for this second level. To what human need does this First Archetype correspond? Which need is so completely First Archetype that with its absence nothing else is possible? It is survival. Without continued existence, then love, justice, relationship, law—all of it—simply isn't feasible.

This makes the next level rather easy to describe, and it's easy to see how it flows directly from the first two. What attitudes, moods and behaviors run forth from the above? It's a quality of belligerence   a feistiness, a chip-on-the-shoulder attitude. You can see how anger and rage fit in. On the first two levels, you can also see there is a neutrality. Here, on this level, there is a definite gamut that moves from good to evil, from functional to dysfunctional, from appropriate to inappropriate, and from integrated to un-integrated.

Let's play with the full range a bit. Examples of this negative-to-positive scope might include: cruel, mean, angry, belligerent, thoughtless, artless, active, risk-loving, energetic, athletic, lively, joyful.

On the next level, we have the thousand things of the world, and they are truly endless. I'll mention a few to give you an idea how to explore this further: a sword, a fight, a soldier, a penis, machismo, RAM(bo). Of course, these are the most obvious. But you can see and feel how these thousand things have their source in the Cosmic Principle and how this Principle infuses each and every one of them. Go back to the beginning and feel how the Cosmic Principle of Assertion has its direct expression in the fundamental Human Need of Survival. Feel how that precipitates moods, attitudes and behaviors described by the words such as quick-tempered, fierce, hot-blooded, vigorous, impulsive, etc. Feel how fights, knives, soldiers, brutes, etc. are further expressions of this.

After you have moved on past the First Archetype to complete your exploration of all twelve of the Archetypes— when you have your own evolving list of concepts—it will become obvious how these, each in turn, relate to one another in precise astrological ways. How is the First Archetype Principle diametrically opposed, yet complimentary, to the Seventh? How do the Fourth, the Eighth and the Twelfth Archetypal Needs flow into each other, and why? The answer to these and other such questions will be on the tip of your tongue by the time our exploration of the Archetypes is complete. What we're doing is beginning to translate the Astro-Logos—the language of Astrology—into English.

There is nothing in this study that does not partake of these principles, either singly or in combination. Seeing this—seeing how the astrological moment is synchronous with what it brings into existence—is what makes the effective, mature astrologer, one who completely understands that every moment of life is rich with astrological significance!

Nothing brought this to mind more succinctly for me than a lecture I heard once by Dennis Elwell. In Mr. Elwell's lecture, he listed several objects that combined the energy of Saturn (time, age, rocks, boundaries, antiques, harshness, restrictions, cold, limitations, discipline, hardships, endurance) with the energy of Neptune ("spirits" of all sorts, poisons, delusions, secrets, confusion, music, dissolving, spiritual ideals, feet and oil). When I heard this lecture, I had one of those "Ah Ha!" experiences—it wasn't that I was unaware of the diversification of astrological keywords; it was that I now heard it articulated in an absolutely ingenious way. At the time, I took some cryptic notes, which means that the following is paraphrased. Nevertheless, I shall share what I have so that you too can see just how diversified a combination of astrological keywords—or archetypal energies—can be.

To begin, let's take Saturn along with Neptune's association with the sea. There are sea anchors, sea blockades, lost at sea, burial at sea, icebergs, frozen fish, eroding coastlines, fishing limits, sea walls, marine geology, marine archeology, long and tiresome voyages.

Now, remembering some of Neptune's keywords, let's look at some simplistic, mundane implications in viewing Saturn's association with time. That combination could include things like old violins, those moments when time vanishes into an enigmatic obscurity, older people who are invalids, worn shoes, phony antiques, age-old ideals, aged liquors, the melting watches of Salvador Dali.

Then, keeping in mind the diversities of the keywords, we could add rocky coasts, remote islands, solitary drinking, the narcotics squad, taxes on gasoline, lead poisoning in gasoline (which came into social focus when Neptune went into Capricorn), cool wine cellars, a secret garden with a wall around it, wet suits, organized chaos —like building sites, and confused boundary lines.

To totally integrate astrology into your consciousness, try the following exercise. It is quite beneficial.

Observe characters in a play, movie or TV, look
at books on a bookshelf, and categorize situations
and/or objects in light of their astrological
correspondences. User warning: This type of
"play" is extremely addictive!

Now, the conclusion I want to make is that it would be impossible to record every combination of keywords and countless implications; there has to be a better way to clarify these basic human conditions. And, of course, there is. The way our particular species has passed on their internal wisdoms throughout the ages is through story telling, better known as mythology. If a picture is worth a thousand words, then a myth, or allegory, is worth a thousand pictures. Joseph Campbell discloses that myth is a secret opening which energies can flow into the manifestation of human culture. He says: *Religions, philosophies, arts, the social forms of primitive and historic man, prime discoveries in science and technology, the very dreams that blister sleep, boil up from the basic, magic ring of myth.*

Another view of that concept comes from Liz Greene in her *Astrology of Fate*. There, she takes mythology's purpose into the paradigm of the archetype by relating the Greek word "mythos" to its two separate meanings: *"In one sense, mythos is a story. In another, more profound sense, it implies a scheme or plan. It is this latter shading of the word that is most relevant both to psychology and astrology..."* because, she said, that the *"basic mythic motifs reveal a ground plan or purposeful pattern of development inherent in the human psyche as well as in the human body."* She believes that the lives of both individuals and nations are not random, *"nor shaped exclusively by environmental factor..."* She thinks there is definite intention, or "teleology" which corresponds to patterning factors in the psyche that Jung called "archetypes..."

So, what I am launching into with the material that follows is to take the metaphoric implications of the astrological energies into the exploration of our mythological foundation—by introducing traditional mythology to that which relates to these archetypes—while also exploring modern insinuations that the myths suggest.

Chapter **4**

The First Archetype

Mars —Aries -First House
Fire- Cardinal- Angular

The First Archetype. The beginning. It's where the Sun rises —
where it rises in the east each morning; and as well, where it rises
over the Equator at the Vernal Equinox to bring back warmth and
growth in the northern hemisphere: the First House, the first sign,
Aries.

Orphic Hymn 65 to Ares, translation by Taylor from *Wikipedia*,
the free encyclopedia:

> "*To Ares, Fumigation from Frankincense. Mag-
> nanimous, unconquered, boisterous Ares, in darts
> rejoicing, and in bloody wars; fierce and untamed,
> whose mighty power can make the strongest walls
> from their foundations shake: mortal-destroying*

king, defiled with gore, pleased with war's dreadful and tumultuous roar. Thee human blood, and swords, and spears delight, and the dire ruin of mad savage fight. Stay furious contests, and avenging strife, whose works with woe embitter human life; to lovely Kyrpis [Aphrodite] and to Lyaios [Dionysos] yield, for arms exchange the labours of the field; encourage peace, to gentle works inclined, and give abundance, with benignant mind."

Myths do not originate within a particular culture but instead transform their identity into each of the cultures, adapting to each one's traditional needs. The core archetypal essence, however, remains the same. Anyone casually acquainted with Western mythology can witness this transition from the Greek God of War, Ares, into the Roman Pantheon as Mars. Nonetheless, identification of both of these gods—Greek or Roman—is evident throughout the ages; although the form changes, the essence remains the same. Moreover, the primordial evidence of this archetype is secure in every mammal's social structure: into our cousins—the primates, into dogs and cats, and into possums and sea lions. Every mammal can relate to this archetype: the competitive, combative, vying focus of masculine supremacy.

Don't, however, let the word masculine confuse you into thinking that we are referring to boys. This is the assertive outward drive toward autonomy, toward breaking free into becoming an individual, but not yet individuation. That doesn't come at this level; nonetheless, this energy does represent the drive to move toward it. It's the energy that separates. It's not very social, yet it's very essential.

Ares in Greek mythology was real scum. He took machismo to an all-time high. Indeed, he was The God of War, but he did it with a Steven King flair—much more Scorpionic. He roamed the battlefields mutilating bodies, severing body parts, and drinking blood. He was mean and cruel, and he showed no mercy. He smelled badly, and he wasn't a deity one personally wanted to get too close to—except when one was really very angry—destructively angry.

Ares, according to Wikipedia, was the Greek god of war. The son of Zeus and Hera (Rome's Jupiter and Juno, respectively) was one of the Twelve Olympians and even though he was their god of war, he was more accurately *the physical or violent aspect of war...," "...overwhelming, insatiable in battle, destructive, and man-slaughtering."* He was the root of every conflict, according to Greek mythology, but mainly he was the significant god of all weapons of war, the defense, as well as the sacking of cities. Too, his energy was attributed to banditry, manliness and courage.

In Liz Greene's *Astrology of Fate* there was a distinct comparison between the "winged heaven-gods (mental gods)" and the more primitive urges symbolized by Ares. She supposes that the "*violence and passion of Ares are frightening to a civilised ego, and are easily cut off and 'banished to Tartaros'—in other words, repressed.*" She saw this as a potentially painful issue because Mars (in one's chart) is tied up with the confidence in one's vitality, courage and self-determination. Ares is connected to fertility, as well as survival, both biologically and psychically and the repudiation of Mars, because of his primitiveness can often result in a sense of powerlessness—and impotence.

The passage of Ares' archetypal image into the Roman Mars is an interesting transition. They extended Ares' image to fit with an already established deity of agriculture and fruitfulness. This transition into the Roman culture gave a diverse archetypal suggestion to this god. The Greeks were intellectuals; logical rationalism was the basis of their culture. Within my observation, it seems that the Greek culture was much more aware of the fundamental baseness of human nature. This is obviously reflected in Ares, upon whom they could project and identify their brutality.

Rome, on the other hand, with its gentler god of war and aggression, produced a brutal culture, one that delighted in forcing slaves to take weapons and fight one another to the death at their own grave sites. The popularity of gladiatorial combat is another testament to the awesome brutality of Roman culture. The first known combat between gladiators in Rome was held at the funeral of Marcus Brutus in 264 BCE, and from there it became popular, the most macabre spectator sport in the history of Western civilization. It is reported that Emperor Titus staged one grisly show that lasted one hundred days; on another occasion, Emperor Trajan celebrated a military victory by displaying five thousand pairs of gladiators. Roman writers recorded that the bloodshed in the arena was often so great that the contest would have to be interrupted, to allow resurfacing of the slippery fighting area with clean sand. Gladiatorial schools were a great business, and even though the few successful gladiators were national heroes, most of their ranks were made up of slaves, criminals and prisoners of war, who were recruited against their will. The demand for gladiators was often so great that innocent people were shanghaied or imprisoned. Such people were rarely qualified, even after training, and most were slain in the arena.

Gladiatorial schools were not the only vocation that prospered, however. Both male and female prostitutes were housed on the first floor underneath the arenas. The sexual energy was so great that it was necessary to provide personal relief for the spectators.

(Ares at his best!)

Now, let's take a detour from Greece and Rome to look at the physical planet Mars. It is speculated that in an earlier time, Mars the planet was much more like earth; however possibly most of the planet's carbon dioxide was used up. This formed carbonate rocks. It seems that Mars lacks tectonic plates and is unable to recycle any of this carbon dioxide back into its atmosphere. This prohibits it from sustaining the necessary 'greenhouse effect.'

Like our planet, Mars has icy poles and there is evidence of erosion that clearly indicates that water once ran over its surface –which is speculated to have been about four billion earth years ago. Though somewhat similar, there are also several differences. One is, as I've mentioned above, that Mars' apparently lacks tectonic plates since there's no evidence of horizontal motion of the surface, such as folded mountains that are so common on earth. This may account for its violent volcanoes; its lack of a global magnetic field; and its thin atmosphere. Also it's capable of supporting very strong winds and vast dust storms that on occasion engulf the entire planet for months. Yet another difference is that it's possible Mars' core is solid. In addition to its ample amounts of iron and iron sulfide, in all likelihood it contains a relatively large fraction of sulfur.

All of these characteristics have subsequently given Mars the name of "The Angry Red Planet." Therefore, it can be concluded that the physical planet is a metaphor for the archetype. Since Mars is unable to recycle its carbon dioxide, that would, in essence, not allow the planet to sustain life. Carbon dioxide is a poison gas (or residue of energy) that must be recycled in order to sustain life. Maintaining the metaphor, one must be willing to "recycle" this archetypal energy to sustain one's life. Anger becoming stagnant is deadly.

Sexuality that is not expressed openly and healthily can be condensed into perversion. It is necessary to acknowledge this archetypal energy with respect, or the culture (or individual) will manifest a brutal environment. When a culture suppresses this primal expression, that culture projects rage onto the society. Our culture certainly can fit into one that requires a projection. Individually, we find these Arian/Martian urges abhorrent. This is exactly why our sports players make more money than almost anyone else in our society. It is also why we look at the gangs in our inner cities and click our tongues, because it is no more than our own cesspool of anger that we project through a vehicle of prejudice. Through the vicarious venue of the television evening news, we can brutally rape, cruelly murder, and plunder with an amoral flair. The continuing themes of our movies reflect our insatiable desire for blood, fear, and pain.

This archetypal repression has also been revealed as a cause of the disease of cancer, and it is possibly the reason why cancer is such a popular killer within our society. According to many health-care authorities, cancer is suppressed rage that our mind (or consciousness) rejects and puts within our solid core—the body. (The First Archetype begins the First Quadrant, which is associated with unconscious, primal development, and as well, one of the major keywords for the First House is the body.) I've known many people who have lost a loved one to cancer say that they were the "sweetest people" they'd ever known. Perhaps this is the source of the aphorism, "Only the good die young."

Both Ares and Mars were children from the marriage of Zeus/Hera (Greek) or Jupiter/ Juno (Roman). At close scrutiny, this marriage is stereotypical of Western culture's dysfunctional relationship (which we'll go into in more detail with the Seventh Archetype).

Again, we are faced with the Greek's version of realism over Rome's idealism. In the Greek version, the relationship of Hera and Zeus was overtly more dysfunctional than in the Roman; subsequently, as any mental health person could predict, Ares' anti-social behavior was imminent. He was Hera's favorite son, indicating the likelihood of her making him her surrogate mate, especially in light of Zeus' promiscuity.

Zeus, on the other hand, rejected Ares and would have nothing to do with him. Caustically, he called him "Hera's son." Ares and his only sibling, Hephaistos (more gentle, but crippled and ugly, and rejected by his mother), were tormented by their parent's constant bickering. Moreover, their parents insisted that they choose sides. There-after, characteristically Ares was unable to acquire an intimate relationship, holding the whole institution of marriage in contempt. On the other hand, when he was not drinking his conquest's blood, he was busy defeating the virtues of females—both mortal and immortal. His main consort, however, was Aphrodite/Venus: his pitiable brother's wife!

The realness of this archetypal image of Ares is quite evident in our culture. Alters and sacrifices to this god are evident. One can view the many devoted worshippers in front of the television on Monday nights during football season. Then, go into any of our single bars. Additionally, the circumstances around this development are skillfully perpetrated within the family structures.

Liz Greene quotes Te Paske in the *Astrology of Fate* who speaks about the issues of rape and Ares' obvious rage against Hera. In his interpretation, he says that in the theme of rape, Mars is the figure which *"embodies the brute, warlike and aggressive nature of man standing opposed to, and yet in love with, Aphrodite."* Te Paske goes on to quote Jung as saying that Mars may be considered as *"the principle of individuation in the strict sense."* This position of 'strict sense' would denote, according to Te Paske, *"the individuating principle as hot, violent sulphurous..."* much like the physical attributes of the physical planet, Mars. *"Mars represents power and anger in rudimentary and concrete form..."*

Liz concludes by saying, *"...Mars within a woman is no different from Mars within a man; it is the urge to actualise one's individual identity in the world."*

If mythology tells an archetypal story, then the physical world tells a metaphorical story. As insinuated by Liz Greene's quotation from Te Paske, the physical composition of the planet Mars can easily be metaphorical. Mars, the planet, is both cold and dry, with two moons. As mentioned above, at one time there was clearly water on the planet's surface, and that would metaphorically indicate that in a forgotten past, emotion/transformation was a part of its formation. Its surface shows a harsh aridness that certainly matches its mythological character.

As well, Mars is our second closest neighbor (Venus being our first); however, out of all our brother and sister planets of the solar system, Mars is the one whose composition is most like that of earth. That is definitely symbolic! Perhaps as we move closer to integrating our primal urges into individuation, we will actually colonize Mars.

Now, this brings us back into the beginning: the Sun rising in the east every morning, to the Sun coming above the Equator every year. With one we enter a day; with the other we enter a new seasonal year. Likewise, when we are born, we enter a new physical (Earth-suit) body. And as we cross over into that physical body, we enter a new lifetime. It matters not which we maintain—

reincarnation or one lifetime for redemption—we are nonetheless currently dealing with this one specific lifetime. It's the contract we sign at birth: [with right hand raised] I DO SOLEMNLY SWEAR TO BE THIS INDIVIDUAL [insert name here] FOR THE DURATION OF THIS LIFETIME, TO THE VERY BEST OF MY ABILITY.

The First Archetype depicts our individuality—the baby being born: "I'm here, I have a right to be here, I have needs and I want them met NOW!" Subsequently, it also represents one's personal, physical space on this planet. Is that not the major focus of war: taking someone else's space? Killing someone is eliminating their space and their individuality.

Nonetheless, how can one respect my space if he doesn't respect his own?

Our anger and our individuation are only the periphery of this archetype. Its core maintains its position throughout this material, and that core is male sexuality. As I expressed close to the outset, the current mythology is the resurrection of an older belief system. Ares came forth from the waning of other male deities. Somewhere between here and there, we've lost Mars' true focus. We not only lost the original focus of this archetypal energy, but it fell into abasement as well.

For millennia, creation and copulation were synonymous. During those times, the phallic was revered, beautifully and reverently. In mythology, there are always the myths of creation. Some of these stories tell of both male and female copulating their origin; however, in some, only the female principle is recognized while in others (such as the one which follows), only the male.

I will paraphrase a story told in ancient Egyptian mythology that says, "When I had come into being, being itself came into being; and all things came into being after I came into being. I was the one who copulated with my hand, and then I spewed out of my 'mouth' that which was Tefnut …" continuing on and on until the entire Egyptian pantheon was birthed.

Ancient Sumer was situated in the Tigris/Euphrates valley, known as the cradle of civilization. In that culture they used the same word for water and for rain and for semen. Think of what it would be like in our culture if the word for semen was the same as the word for water!

Think of the masculine principle, and the archetype of creation—of becoming—as one and the same. As we go through a birthing process, there are many archetypal images of Ares, bloody being just one. Ultimately, we must embrace and honor all the implications of our First Archetype if we wish to be. Trying to live a life without Mars is impossible, for what it generates is energy, just like the winds of the physical planet. Trying to live one's life while denying Mars can only bring one's demise, for it is the fountainhead of living.

Chapter **5**

The Second Archetype

Venus~Taurus~Second House, Earth~Fixed~ Succedent

In the beginning the story goes something like this: There was Gaia, who was the Mother of the Earth, while Uranus was the Father of the Sky. Their children were the forefathers of the beautiful Olympian gods; they were the monstrous Titians – huge, horrible and hideous. As each was to be born, Ouranous (Uranus) would shove the ugly infant back into Gaia's belly. The father's rejection created quite a resentment from the offspring.

(Now this tells an important, archetypal story...The sky represents intellect, while the earth is instinctual. So the battle begins...)

Finally Gaia had had enough, and when her youngest son was born—Cronos (Saturn)—she provided him with a stone sickle, which he used to castrate Uranus, throwing his member into the sea. (The debt of the son who becomes his mother's surrogate mate! Keep this image in mind when you get to the Tenth Archetype and Saturn's energy.)

Drops of blood fell to earth, and from those drops sprung the Erinyes, or Furies. They were the three goddesses of vengeance—Tisiphone (avenger of murder), Megaers (the jealous) and Alecto (constant anger). The Furies would punish all crime, striking the offenders with madness. Without mercy they would penalize all who broke the rules and never stopped following criminals.

From the foam produced by Uranus's testicles, et al, which fell into the stormy sea, grew a girl. The waves surrounded her, lifting her up and carrying her first to Kythera and then to Cyprus. There the lovely goddess stepped forth with her two companions, Eros, whose name means love and Himeros, whose name means desire. Where her feet touched the earth, grass grew. Her name to mortals was Aphrodite, which means born from foam. She was the goddess belonging to all people. It is said that she is present in whispering girls, smiles and seductions, and all sweet delights. She was welcomed on Olympus by the gods and goddesses (even though she was an offspring of Gaia and Uranus), where she ruled the procreation of all living things, art and beauty.

Homeric Hymn to Aphrodite

I will sing of stately Aphrodite, gold-crowned and beautiful, whose dominion is the walled cities of all sea-set Cyprus. There the moist breath of the western wind wafted her over the waves of the loud-moaning sea in soft foam, and there the gold-filleted Hours welcomed her joyously. They clothed her with heavenly garments: on her head they put a fine, well-wrought crown of gold, and in her pierced ears they hung ornaments of orichalc and precious gold, and adorned her with golden necklaces over her soft neck and snow-

white breasts, jewels which the gold- filleted Hours wear themselves whenever they go to their father's house to join the lovely dances of the gods. And when they had fully decked her, they brought her to the gods, who welcomed her when they saw her, giving her their hands. Each one of them prayed that he might lead her home to be his wedded wife, so greatly were they amazed at the beauty of violet-crowned Cytherea.

(ll. 19-21) Hail, sweetly-winning, coy-eyed goddess! Grant that I may gain the victory in this contest, and order you my song. And now I will remember you and another song also.

To the ancient Greeks, Aphrodite was their "golden goddess." Never in Western history has a Goddess had such recognition or been more illustrated than Aphrodite/Venus. The Greeks regarded their sexuality as a sacred gift, and nothing delights Aphrodite more than the gratification of the senses. Moreover, she wasn't denied the rule of any living thing, for Venus/ Aphrodite was, and is—in all things—the sensuous presence.

This primal energy has been present, and recognized as present, from the onset of life. Since the beginning of human civilization, she has had many names: Venus, Aphrodite, Cybele, Hathor. As civilization formed in the Tigris/Euphrates valley, and mythology was established in Sumer's social structure, this archetypal energy permeated their lives as Ishtar. Later, she evolved into Babylon's Astarte.

The more matriarchal societies experienced her as a goddess of sensual reproduction. This station elevated her to the supreme queen of heaven. Between 3000 and

1800 BCE, there were temples where Ishtar was served by her priestesses, the qadishtu. The socially sanctified activities of these women were to participate freely in sexual and sensual rituals. For centuries, such temples were commonplace in the Western world, forming an essential aspect of matriarchal society, one that we can hardly imagine today. The patriarchal tribes of Israel (who were in exile, as well) had difficulty reconciling the goddess worship they encountered. Their patriarchs and prophets rarely missed an opportunity to debase Astarte-Ishtar as "the great Whore of Babylon."

Such practices were not just prevalent in the Middle Eastern area of Africa, however. They were present in early Greek/European traditions as well. According to Merlin Stone, in *When God Was A Woman*, women celebrated the Feast of Adonis at the temple of Aphrodite in Corinth by having one-night stands with the stranger of their choice as late as 150 AD. Between the Greeks and us, however, stands Christianity. As pointed out earlier in this text, the Judeo-Christian tradition defiled the feminine mystique. Subsequently, its followers would certainly find a religion that honored Aphrodite's liberal love of the body and appreciation of sensuous sexual pleasure, horrifying!

These concepts were heightened through the later ministry of the Roman citizen, Saul— a.k.a. Saint Paul—who aspired to project his negative obsession with fornication. In fact, in his eyes the only purpose for marriage was that it was *"better to marry than to burn* [in lust]" (I Corinthian 7:9). To him, celibacy was the only superior position; and his proclamations definitely reduced copulation down to necessary procreation. And please! no pleasure involved! The Moslems—succedent of the Christians—have gone so far as to mutilate their young females' clitoris to make certain there will never be pleasure.

Interestingly enough, there is no evidence that Jesus either looked down on women or abominated sex. It was not in any of the alleged teachings of Jesus that sexual practice be banned. If anything, he supported women's rights, and there is indication that he had close women followers. Actually, a legend/myth, which came out of the Dark Ages and has not gotten much press over the centuries, claims that Mary Magdalene was pregnant with Jesus' child at the time of his death. The story goes on to tell of her flight, along with a group of devoted followers, into France. Some today believe that the search for the Holy Grail was actually the search for Mary Magdalene and Jesus' child or children, those being the holy vessel or cup for Jesus' blood. For a fascinating account of this, I heartily recommend the book *Holy Blood, Holy Grail* by Michael Baigent.

Needless to say, because of Paul (Roman Saul, the true initiator of global Christianity) and others of like mind, who obviously feared the power of the feminine mystique, we have spent the larger part of two millennia trying to annihilate the essence of this feminine archetype. But unlike many of the other goddesses of the pantheon, Venus cannot be annihilated. To the Christian fathers a seductive woman is the epitome of sin. Christianity's stance toward Venus has brought true meaning to the adage, "Can't live with her and can't live without her." And in spite of patriarchal control, shame, guilt, punishment, and death, her archetypal energy within humanity is too primordial to eradicate.

Venus is the archetypal metaphor for the primordial essence of femininity. All archetypal energies are primal, but at this point I am making a definite distinction between the words primal and primordial. Within this context, I postulate that "primordial" means cellular instincts among mammals—or in this case, among all living things; when I say primal, however, I mean indigenous instincts to humans. Subsequently, to obliterate this Venus icon would be to terminate life on this planet (a situation that is presently becoming a serious concern), for Venus is the archetype of fertile vigor—the productive force—in every domain on this planet, wherever life exists.

(This is synchronously reflected in the Greek myth: She was the daughter of Uranus, the earliest Sky-God, and came into manifestation as a sibling of Cronos (Saturn)—before the "birth" of Zeus, his siblings, and offspring.)

The First and the Second Archetypes form a unit in this regard. In terms of ancient rulership, this is apparent as well. Mars rules Aries, Venus rules Taurus, Venus rules Libra, and Mars rules Scorpio. So one follows the other, as well as opposes the other. They form a polarity as well as a duo. It is interesting to consider that in mythology these two are not married (probably a good choice). They are, however, quite energetic lovers, and mythology is replete with stories of their escapades.

Mars penetrates, Venus engulfs. Mars asserts, Venus attracts. The Mars force is Centrifugal; the Venus force is Centripetal. They are both primal and primordial. One or the other is neither good nor bad, neither positive nor negative. They can both go overboard to ones detriment. Only by balancing and consciously integrating the two antagonistic energies can an entity grow.

The psychological consequences of the subsequent religious concoction of femme fatale in our culture have harvested very black, shadowy outcomes. Initially it resulted in widespread paranoia around feminine wisdoms and arts, culminating in the execution of witches as an end result. It then produced sexual dysfunction and neuroses of such magnitude as to make us totally disconnected from whatever may be wholesome; it has given our social system a deleterious attitude concerning money and possessions; and lastly, an outgrowth of this femme fatale persuasion has nearly destroyed the planet with the rejection of feminine affinities. (Even now, as we enter the twenty-first century, it is more acceptable for a woman to "be" like a man, than it is for a man to "be" like a woman.)

Nonetheless, it is not possible to be totally free from the feminine archetypal expression. Prudently, the Christian fathers allowed weak portrayals of the feminine through Mother Mary and Mary Magdalene—the Mother and the Whore. Mary Magdalene became Venus' counterpart and carried the patriarchal hope of redemption for her primal turmoil; and the portrayal of the Moon is the unfruitful Mother Mary, who bore a child without carnal knowledge. However, replacing real women with the worship of Mary is seen as a major setback for men's psychological development. In a range of writings by Carl Jung, he thought it was especially damaging in the area of relationships, subsequently distracting attention from the virtues of real women. But there is an even grimmer consequence of this repression: the awakening in men's unconscious of the witch archetype. Jung felt that the depreciation of the "real woman" was compensated by impulses from the unconscious by demonic impulses and projected upon the object. Man loves woman less as a result of this depreciaton and hence she appears to him as a witch. Thus, the delusion about witches—that ineradicable blot upon the Later Middle Ages—developed along with, and indeed as a result of, the intensified worship of the Virgin.

So, the true essence of Venus has become a slut in our world. The sense of her anger and insecurity are experienced within the portrayal of Snow White's wicked stepmother. She has indeed given us The Apple, which is indeed full of poison, and it has put us all to sleep. From her archetypal Mirror on the Wall, she ravishes retaliation upon her patriarchal oppressors: she sells products to people who do not need them, or cannot afford them—her seduction permeates our entire commercial world. She crawls in and out of the politician's or evangelist's mind and hotel rooms while she smirks at the forceful destruction that the scandals generate. She strikes terror into the hearts of aging women who find a wrinkle or develop a bulge. And she hides in the closet of every living human within this culture and torments him or her with whispered longings for sexual fulfillment. The Bill Clinton-Monica Lewinsky-Hillary Clinton episode is very much along these lines.

In many reports of the scandal, Clinton was portrayed as the wronged male, preyed upon by a nubile, sex-hungry seductress who crossed into the sacred marriage and took him unwillingly to her bed. This scenario played out well into our culture's lust for the suppressed Aphrodite Archetype. It has all the characters necessary for the appropriate drama: the aging woman—Hillary, and the young seductress—Monica, both bringing society's most powerful male, Bill—the leader of the world at that time—to his knees with their voluptuary and wrath. The Western world loved it! It was the focus of everyday life with its scandal of huge proportions. Obviously we couldn't get enough of it: television, magazines, books—and all this while as a culture, we professed that we didn't care what went on behind closed doors!

What Fire has created, Earth brings into materialization. As the First Archetype spews forth his seed of creative manifestation, the Second takes the creative force into the security of her fertile, moist bed of rhapsody. If the First is the birth into the physical Earth-world, then the Second is the allegiance with the physical Earth-world. From the lap of the Second Archetype, we make assessments concerning our world —what tastes secure or scary, what feels secure or scary, what smells secure or scary, what sounds secure or scary, and what looks secure or scary. A baby clutching a security blanket, perhaps sucking its thumb, or tickling the end of its nose with a soft, fuzzy corner is a perfect metaphor for the Second Archetype. The list can go on and on. It's the taste of cold ice-cream on the tongue, the feel of cool grass on the bottoms of your feet on a hot summer day, the smell of fresh rain, the sight of someone you love getting off an airplane, the sound of your favorite song, the ecstasy of being turned-on sexually, the feel of silk, swimming nude, or a massage. Or even taking a bath. Bathing was considered indecent and highly immoral because of the Roman bath. The Roman people were incredibly clean people; however, their baths were mostly public. I'm sure that the public baths could easily be taken into sensuality—a very Second Archetype delight!

In the way that the First Archetype is pure masculinity, it is of course obvious that the Second Archetype is pure femininity. Nonetheless, it goes beyond that. The First Archetype is the only one that is purely the essence of masculinity; and Second Archetype is the only one that is purely feminine. All the other archetypal energies may lean to one side or the other (especially directed by their positive and negative persuasion), but they are at least androgynous. The substance that makes a little boy a little boy is the First Archetype, and the substance that makes a little girl a little girl is the Second Archetype. Please note: the above has absolutely nothing to do with socialization! My granddaughter was born a girl; my grandson is a boy. On the other hand, socialization can certainly bring shame and/or denial to the expression of this energy—or it can manipulate its portrayal.

It is very important to claim our First and Second Archetypal expressions. If not, they will be internalized and become our enemies. The First can work with its polarity (the Seventh) and initiate co-dependent behaviors: we can either project our Mars, becoming victims of physical abuse, or we can put our hands on the tops of Ares' head, pushing him down, repressing him, until he explodes our insides into a murderous rage, and we cut deeply with a sharp tongue while we spit vile poison out of our mouth.

Venus thwarted, on the other hand, can drive us to use our seduction on innocent prey, angry that she holds no place of honor. She has us eating ice cream, or chocolate—things that our bodies do not want or need. She has us engaging in sex with people who have no names or personal value. She makes us envious, petty, and small.

Both of these first two archetypes are completely primal and will find expression. Because they are primal, they live in the subconscious and are capable of sabotaging our lives. The only way to eliminate neurotic behavior (that behavior that keeps us out of balance with our conscious motives) is to totally recognize our primal drives—to recognize their needs. To recognize their needs is to actively honor these deities and give them healthy expression in our lives.

Chapter 6

The Third Archetype

Mercury~ Gemini ~ Third House Air~Mutable~Cadent

Homeric Hymn to Hermes, this translation, by Evelyn-White, is in the public domain.

> *"(ll. 1-9) I sing of Cyllenian Hermes, the Slayer of Argus, lord of Cyllene and Arcadia rich in flocks, luck-bringing messenger of the deathless gods. He was born of Maia, the daughter of Atlas, when she had made with Zeus, -- a shy goddess she. Ever she avoided the throng of the blessed gods and lived in a shadowy cave, and there the Son of Cronos used to lie with the rich- tressed nymph at dead of night, while white-armed Hera lay bound in sweet sleep: and neither deathless god nor mortal man knew it.*

(ll. 10-11) And so hail to you, Son of Zeus and Maia;
with you I have begun: now I will turn to another
song!"
(l. 12) Hail, Hermes, giver of grace, guide, and giver
of good things! (31)

The Third Archetype is, of course, the planet Mercury, the
Third House, and the sign of Gemini. It should be immediately
stressed that the Third Archetype has been grossly trivialized in
western contemporary astrology. This is because of an absolutely
misguided perception about this Archetype. Many astrologers
see Mercury in a chart and say something trivial. Generally they
start talking about the lower mind, and something pertaining
to communication—letter writing, talking on the telephone,
gossiping. The Third House is siblings and short journeys and
early education. Most astrologers start to throw out the basic
astrological keywords at this point and begin to amble off in some
directionless haze, interpreting the Third vaguely, in a Neptunian
manner.

There is, however, nothing trivial about Mercury or the
Third Archetype. It's no accident that esoteric astrology places
Mercury as the ruler of Aries. As we know from the First
Archetype, Aries holds the essence of a vanguard. This promotes
Mercury to a totally different perception. This suggests that he is
a trail-blazer.

In the Judeo/Christian Bible, the very first words are,
"In the beginning was the WORD." Word, in this context relates
to Logos…the Higher Principle, or, Concept. It is an important
dynamic. Mercury is often mistaken as trivial because of its
flexibility and versatility; this can be seen in its rulership of two
mutable signs. But mistaking the mercurial for the trivial is a
serious error.

First of all, it is necessary to realize that the placement
of this archetype is still within the First Quadrant, and this
quadrant is primal and entirely subjective. If the depiction of the
First Archetype is "the baby being born" and the image for the

Second Archetype is "the baby sensing," then the Third is "the baby conceptualizing." The First Quadrant establishes the proper space into which to fit these first three processes. Everything flows perfectly from what came before.

Another way of saying a baby being born would be to say that an entity is coming into the earth's corporeal, material reality. Another way of saying a baby is sensing would be to say that an entity is susceptible to a corporeal reality. And, another way to say a baby is conceptualizing would be to say that this new entity is classifying the sensations of this corporeal reality. Therefore, these are the subjective concepts of one's immediate environment, and they are integral to the entity's primary development.

Actually, the portrayal of the god Mercury fits into a very similar position within the pantheon as does Venus, and like her, he too is quite primeval. Tracing mythological Mercury back takes us to the onset of the most ancient of culture, Egypt. The Egyptian god, Thoth (Thot) was the patron of wisdom, the arts, and speech; he was the inventor of hieroglyphics and science; and he was the author of the *Book of the Dead*. He was also known as Tehuti.

Oftentimes with these mythological characters, one sees the polarity, in this case the Third and the Ninth. Like all polarities, there is no difference in the energy, but rather a difference in how the energy is acted out. In this characterization, Thoth was The Measurer, and The Judge (which relates to the Ninth), and Weprehewy, who presided over Horus, after he engaged in the great battle with his uncle Set to avenge his father Osiris' death.

Within Egypt's most ancient culture, he was the heart and tongue of the Sun god, Ra.

Following closely behind—and sometimes referenced interchangeably—is the Greek Hermes. His father was Zeus and his mother was Maia. Hermes' cunning was evident from the very on-set, for on the morning of his birth he got up and went out of his cave and stole his brother Apollo's cows. He made them walk backward so to obscure the direction. Then he killed a tortoise, stringing the shell with reeds, making the first lyre. A shepherd saw what the baby had done and told Apollo. Apollo appealed to Zeus for justice; however, when Hermes played his lyre, the music was so enchanting that it appeased Apollo, his anger dissipated and he allowed Hermes to keep the cattle. Apollo gave Hermes a golden winged staff, an instrument empowered to produce harmony out of discord. Hermes tested the staff by setting it between two fighting serpents and instantly the snakes twisted around the staff in peace. The winged staff with the serpents is called a caduceus.

Hermes is prominent in many of the Greek myths. Originally he was a local fertility god, and he became known as the bringer of wealth. Subsequently, he became the patron of merchants, gamblers, and thieves. Similar to his counterpart Thoth, Hermes was the inventor of the alphabet, mathematics, music, astrology/astronomy, and gymnastics. His symbol, the caduceus, remains the icon of traditional Western medicine today. He is also the mythological founder of alchemy. Hermes was the god of the wind, so subsequently, he and his Roman counterpart, Mercury, rule the breath and lungs. Hermes ruled speed, communication, and thought, and he was the conductor of the souls of the dead to the underworld.

When we follow this deity into Germanic Europe, however, we find one of the most powerful gods in Germanic Mythology. According to the ancient writings, he was grand, above all else, and his mythology was widespread, encompassing all of Western Europe. His assimilation of the characteristics of the old Indo-European Sky Father made him the oldest, as well as the supreme god. The writings of the Roman, P. Cornelius Tacitus (c.55-c.120 AD), in Germania gives the earliest known account of the life and religion of these Germanic tribes. He said that the first people to cross the Rhine to conquer the Gauls were a tribe called Germans and gradually the whole region adapted this name. This name was chosen by the terror it inspired. The main god they worshiped was Mercury and considered it no sin to win his favor on specific days by offering him human sacrifices. They appeased Hercules and Mars with only the animals which were normally allowed.

This account gives evidence of the Mercury and Mars alliance in the primal, First Quadrant. According to C. G. Jung, there are no random circumstances in the higher order of the Collective Unconscious. Everything is the metaphor of another, deeper meaning, if one simply looks. A sacrifice is often demanded by these First Quadrant gods. How often have we demolished something truly dear in our lives with anger; how often has a conscious commitment been disavowed for personal titillation; and haven't we all, at one time or another, sacrificed integrity to rationale?

Nevertheless, the archetypal myth of Mercury permeates all social development. The above-mentioned Germanic deity was developed in primitive northwest Europe. The name can be traced to the far north and to the god, Wodenaz. It became Wuotan in Old High German; then it became Wodan in Old Saxon and Woden in Old English. In Scandinavia, he was first Voden, then Odin in Old Norse.

It was believed that, originally, this god—by whatever name—was a divine magician who, by self-sacrifice, brought wisdom to men. The account below is from the Eddur, poems and tales of Norse mythology, written in 13th century in Iceland, the most complete source for Germanic mythology. In a poem it tells of Odin hanging himself from Yggdrasill—the World Ash Tree that supports the universe in Norse mythology. He hangs there for nine nights, wounded and without food or drink, as 'an offering to himself' to obtain the runes of wisdom. In translation it says, *"And there below I looked; I took up the runes shrieking I took them, And forthwith back I fell...Then began I to thrive and wisdom to get, I grew and well I was; Each word led me on to another word, Each deed to another deed."* As the god of self-sacrifice and wisdom who suffered that man might benefit, he is depicted in the myths as pledging one of his eyes to Mimir in return for the draught of wisdom from Mimir's Well.

Please note this does not indicate that this primordial god sacrificed himself to another, but rather, as "an offering to himself" to obtain knowledge. The mind works within itself, delineating and problem-solving in its subjective world. The mind's wisdom is subjective. Thoughts are processed through one's subjective rationale, subsequently seeking reason in a chaotic world (another view of the polarity of the Third and Ninth Archetypes).

An interesting concept to ponder here is Odin's sacrifice of his eye. At first glance it seems as if Odin allowed one of his two eyes to be plucked out in exchange for wisdom. In Wagner's Ring Cycle, however, Wuotan speaks of giving up his "single" eye. I consider the possible interpretation that Wuotan gave up "single"-eye sight for the human dual eye perspective to gain the wisdom he sought. This also brings up and parallels neatly the duality inherent in Mercury's sign Gemini. In order to gain wisdom, we require the depth-distance perception, yet we also need the awareness of polarity and duality which dual-eye vision implies.

Another interesting concept to ponder is this: An object is not a thing until it has a name. Or, you could say: nothing exists until it has a name. It is a word that makes something a reality.

There is a story told about the travels of James Cook. He tells of his sailing ships anchoring off a Polynesian island. The ships were in plain view from the beaches of the island, sitting majestically upon the horizon; however, the aborigines could not see them. Sailing vessels did not fit into their frame of reality. They could relate to the Long Boats because they had canoes; but the sailing ships were totally invisible. Gradually, their shaman, who could see the boats (because his field of reality was broader) got them to look this way and that way until, one by one, they incorporated that field of reality into their consciousness.

Our reality is based on the perception of thoughts and, subsequently, words. This makes naming a thing a unique process. It is more than we normally consider in our world of prolific words; it pulls the concept of words beyond triviality. Ancient peoples must have been more alert to the significance of this fact; this implication can be seen in the reference of the poem above concerning Odin. The runes were their alphabet, and the runes were sacred. The reading of the runes was considered a prophetic oracle. Of course, the fact that the alphabet was sacred clearly indicates that reading, writing—and perhaps even verbal discourse—were considered sacred as well. To think and then to communicate one's thoughts was as much a breakthrough in the ancient world as the Internet is to us today. This is something that will be pondered in more detail later in this treatise; however, now there is yet another consideration to be made before we can conclude this exploration.

Another facet that has been encountered in every mythological story of Mercury until now is the ability to go into alternate domains, to gather information, and bring it back into this one. In this way, it effectively connects Mercury's mythology to the dual function of the Gemini Twins. These Twins give yet another view of the Mutable/Cadent essence of the Third Archetype.

All cultures seem to have their particular mythological version of Twins. Even going back as far as the Babylonians and Sumerians who came before, they called the constellation we associate with Gemini, the Great Twins, but they did not associate deities or names to them. The Twins are traditional for the archetype of Gemini.

Castor and Polydeuces (Roman Pollux) are the twins who have become traditionally associated with the Constellation of Gemini. Regardless of which twins you are speaking of, when deities were associated with this part of the Zodiac, their story attained a great many complexities; however, the major theme of this story is that one twin is mortal—Castor—while the other, Polydeuces is immortal. Lynceus and Idsa, yet another set of twins, killed Castor during battle. Polydeuces was thoroughly grief-stricken, and went to Zeus, offering to give his life so that his brother might live. Zeus pitied Polydeuces and decreed that the twins would share an alternate life, passing one day beneath the earth in Hades' realm and the next in heavenly Olympus.

"It is traditionally given that Gemini is a moody sign, inclined to swing from elation to depression..." Liz Greene says in **The Astrology of Fate**...*"there is an equilibrium to these opposites,"* she goes on to say. *"Each without the other is incomplete, and the whole personality is dependent upon them*

both. Neither would develop without the other." In other words, it is this duality that creates a whole personality. It is the polarizing experiences of loss/death with the contrasting joy of a divine connection that can bring symmetry to the personality.

If one can manage to become intimate with a person with a Gemini Sun, Moon or Ascendant, they will share with you the depths they go to at times, even though they may never show it outwardly. They have the ability to be on the brink of suicide, but if the phone rings (oftentimes their instrument of choice), their mood seems to swing to the opposite end of the spectrum, and they are able to respond with the most rational voice.

Star Trek's Spock is an excellent example of the Air quality, as well as this specific Archetype. It is not that the Vulcan has no emotions; indeed Spock is extremely emotional during those times when we are allowed to see that side of him. The hallmark of the Vulcan race, though, is that they control their emotional nature.

The Third is the first of the Air signs, but it is still in a Subjective Quadrant—as a matter of fact, it is the primary subjective quadrant. Therefore, it is safe to say that this specific Air sign is totally subjective; yet it is non-judgmental, since Air collects data without discriminating the value of the data. So, what has been said seems to be an oxymoron. It's difficult to understand being subjective while not being discriminating or judgmental. Subsequently, what one is filtering out through the subjective element in this equation is what is perceived as real and what is not.

Our world is perceived through data and our concept of that information. Whatever we perceive is immediately put into a structure, a dimension. That structure is a thought, and we organize our thoughts with words. Then our ability to speak defines us as human beings. If someone has difficulty speaking—defining their reality through speech (recall what we know of Helen Keller's early childhood)—they are discounted and disregarded, somehow considered less than a person, or less of a person. This is a two-way street, however. A child, who has no mental impression of a table, has no perception of the word table. We mentally travel about within our physical world, constantly designing our perceptions through thoughts and organizing these thoughts into words. And within the twin motif, our thoughts can lead us into the darkest despair, or they can take us into the highest heaven.

It is becoming apparent that many people suffer debilitating neurotic malfunctions from traumatic experiences with their siblings, as opposed to only the traumatic experiences brought on by their parents. This Archetype incorporates siblings into the keywords for the Third House. Who else is able to define the many limitations of our corporeal reality better than a sibling's knowing assessments! Through this interaction with the older siblings, we often form our reality. They tell us what is real and not real. Many of us walk through our entire lives limiting our concept of reality by what we were told in adolescence, either by our siblings or our schoolmates in elementary school (another keyword for the Third House is elementary education).

The individual who visualizes a broader concept of reality utilizes the Third Archetype's polarity and brings it down into a subjective view. The Third's polarity—the Ninth—is in the Third Quadrant and is the only Fire that is situated above the Horizon. The Third Quadrant is the most objective Quadrant, since it is composed by the Southern and Western Hemispheres, and is in direct opposition to the First, which, by Hemisphere influence, is the most subjective Quadrant. The archetypal energy of the Third Quadrant is the most difficult to bring into a subjective realm and to make one's own. Nevertheless, if one uses the Ninth Archetype (religion, education, foreign cultures—anything that is a source to broaden one's concept of life), they can take the small pieces of the Third's function and make a large picture that is characteristic of the Ninth. So, working with this idea, we can take some of the concepts that would generally be categorized in the Ninth and give a deeper and more comprehensive image of what one can do, on a fundamental level, with the Third.

There is an article by Michael Thurman in the February/March 1996 *The Mountain Astrologer*, titled *"Astrology and the*

New Physics" that spells out where I'm now going. In this article he tells about a physicist named Max Planck who would make a discovery *"that was to shake the very foundations of science."* While puzzling over the reason that heated metal glows red rather than blue, *"as classical physics would predict, he found that sub-atomic particles don't increase their energy in gradual amounts but in sudden bursts, due to electrons suddenly jumping from one orbit or shell to another."* That discovery was what Planck called 'quanta' and was to lead to the development of quantum theory. This theory states that our universe is *"actually made up of patterns of energy, not atomic particles of 'stuff'."*

Albert Einstein came along, making the whole Quantum concept plausible. *"Einstein's contributions to statistical physics and quantum theory were hardly less significant than those to relativity"* (the 1986 Edition of Collier's Encyclopedia) and Einstein himself once said that he had spent *"a hundred times more thought on quantum problems than on relativity."* Obviously, one affected the other.

Now we know that our physical world is not made up of solid matter, and every school child knows about atoms and that they are the stuff that makes up everything in the universe. Basically, Quantum theory defines atoms and their components; however, an atom is no more solid than our perceived reality. Actually, the only difference between one solid thing and another solid thing is the organization of particular atoms. These atoms are composed of sub-atomic particles, and these particles make up conglomerates of ordered information. And even though we call these things particles, they're not particles either. In the normal sense of the word, they too are impulses of information. The only thing that makes gold different from lead is the arrangement and quantity of these impulses of information. And this may be exactly what the ancient Alchemists already knew.

Quantum physics clearly defines the corporeal world as non-solid material. It is not, however, only non-solid material; it can actually further be defined as comprehending non-solid material. From a lecture by the physicist, Dr. William Keepin, in which he discusses the theory of David Bohm (a colleague of Einstein's), he states that the electron seems to be, *"...essentially acting with a kind of awareness about the rest of the universe. That awareness comes in this second term, which Bohm called the quantum potential, which is a wave-like information field that gives the electron access to information about the rest of the physical universe."*

What we have explored gives us the concept that we have a universe of atoms that acquire and process data; atoms become ordered through impulses of information... and impulses of information are simply thoughts. In other words, the universe thinks.

Our thoughts then are a non-solid concept of a material world. Since a thought is a non-solid concept, it then holds hierarchy over the material world, and we've already determined that a thought shapes our concept of real world. If this is true, then the actuality of the real world is shaped by what we think. Therefore we have actually traveled into the scientific proof of the aphorism "as a man thinketh ...so is he."

After exploring all the attributes of this god, a god who descended through the ages for this archetype, we can attest that these ideas/concepts were nothing new to the midwives, metaphysicians, alchemists, astrologers, and shamans of the ancient world. A god who has the potential, through a thought, to manifest all things—so truly the ancients were correct when they called him the "bringer of prosperity." Even his name, Mercury, seems magical. And Mercury—quicksilver, the metal—was thought to be a magical liquid metal—a fluid, movable god who journeys into a non-solid world, bringing back information for a material world. A god, who through thought, can form a reality.

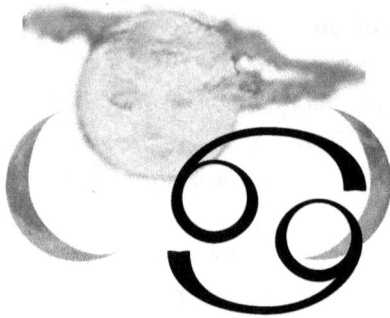

Chapter 7

The Fourth Archetype

Moon~Cancer~Fourth House
Water ~ Cardinal~ Angular

The Fourth House cusp is one of the Angles—one of the intersections of the Ecliptic with another Great Circle, the Meridian. In the northern hemisphere of the earth, it is the Ecliptic crossing the Meridian in the south. If one was in the southern hemisphere, such as Australia, it would be the Ecliptic crossing the Meridian in the north. From the perspective of the viewer and where s/he is standing, the Imum Coeli, "lowest heaven," goes directly through the earth and out the other side. Depending on how far above or below the equator you are standing— remember, the Ecliptic only travels 23° 26-27' above and below the equator—the MC/IC axis will slant a certain number of degrees between the feet. An example would be if a chart was erected for a place in the US state of New Mexico, at the exact same moment in time (Sidereal Time, that is), their IC would be a ship-in-the-Indian-Ocean's MC…and visa versa. The major thing that is being stressed here though, is not where it is, so much as what it is. It goes directly through the earth, so consequently it is your personal "grounding rod." It connects you to the physical experience. As you read the following material, hold that image.

While we hold that image, let me take you back to the Neolithic village—our foundational development as a species. Going back to the earliest period (perhaps c. 7500-3500 B.C.E. in Levat), the main focal figure was the bountiful goddess Earth, as the mother and nurturer of life and the receiver of the dead. All mythological indications point to a mother-goddess who may have been only a local patroness of fertility, as some anthropologists assume. However by the development of higher civilizations (i.e. Sumer, c. 3500-2350 B.C.E.) this focal figure was transformed in to the Great Goddess and temples were built for her worship. Joseph Campbell puts it this way, *"She was…a metaphysical symbol: the arch personification of the power of Space, Time and Matter, within whose bounds all beings arise and die…And everything having form or name—including God personified as good or evil, merciful or wrathful—was her child, within her womb."*

If a mother has a child, and after the birthing of that child, the mother goes off and leaves that child—like on a park bench, or in a garbage can—that child will go back to where it came: it will go back to spirit. Without Mother, we would not, could not, be here. The Mother is the power and the force that brings life into embodiment—from the conception, through the embryonic development, and into maturation. Without enough mothering and/or nurturing, an infant will die. Therefore, all living things had enough mothering…PERIOD. It matters little about personal opinions and complaints; everyone "got enough," or they wouldn't be here.

In Belgium, during WWII, there were so many orphaned and abandoned babies that they had to set up large warehouse-style care to provide for these children's physical needs. They saw that each child was warm and dry, and fed them by propping a bottle up in the crib.

There was not enough staff, however, to hold and cuddle the infants. There were just too many children to give them cooing and cuddling. Before long, an epidemic ran rampant among the babies. Apparently healthy babies were dying of some puzzling infirmity. The autopsy results were even more mysterious. These children, they found, had shriveled-up spines.Their discovery was enigmatic. Finally, they came to realize that the children who were dying were the ones who were lacking physical contact. The children who were getting more physical contact were surviving. Bottom line…one cannot survive without being touched.

Later studies have shown that it doesn't even matter whether the child has negative contact, or positive contact, with the nurturing agent; the results are the same. In other words, a child can have a mother who lavishes affection, or one who screams and beats the child. Short of killing the child, the latter child will survive (or, stay here in the physical world) just as readily as the former child. Oftentimes, the latter child flourishes with equal resolve. Therefore, it is the contact—the physical contact—that brings us into the physical world and grounds us here.

Now, as we come to the end of the first series of action—from Fire into Water—you can see that this is a powerful process, indeed! Reviewing the sequence, we have the Fire that creates, then Earth that stabilizes the creation; Air subsequently conceptualizes the creation, and lastly and ultimately, Water synthesizes the entire process. We can also see that there are three such series of action in the horoscope. We could consider them the Personal, the Social and the Collective. Here, in this Fourth Archetype we've come to the end of the Personal series. Let's take a moment to consider this first foursome. Seen as an entity, how can we synthesize the four? You may find it easier to get a feeling for this quartile pulsation than to find words for it. Trust that feeling and let it guide you. What words could we find to delineate this? How about: Creation, Stabilization, Sustenance, Initial Impulse, Grounding, Communication, Empathy. Think about it.

Please note that, as within the entire astrological paradigm, there is a system within a system: The creation in this particular expression is Cardinal—Aries, and the synthesis is Cardinal—Cancer. Fixed Fire—Leo is the genesis of the next process. The integration of this process is through deep, Watery Scorpio—also Fixed. The same with Mutable: Fire— Sagittarius begins the process, and Water—Pisces ends it. Astrology is demonstrative of order within the Universe—the smallest piece reflects the largest, as one piece reflects yet another piece, and so forth. That's why someone with a limited familiarity of the astrological paradigm can, in fact, give a fairly accurate reading—as long as they stay with generalities.

Within the Fourth Archetype, we can begin to see the manifestation of the synthesis. In addition, we can acquire a deeper meaning within its symbolism. For example, if the First House begins with the symbol of the Sun rising in the East, a birth of the day, then it's obvious that it is symbolic of the birth of the entity. If we are moving from the First for it to be synthesized within the Fourth, and that part of the chart is the only part that goes directly through the earth, then the Fourth House is symbolic of being rooted. Symbolically, it holds physical reality into place. An entity is born into and integrates life's experience through the First, the Mother, and subsequently, the home, the clan, and the community. Within infantile projection, the Mother is not a separate individual, but is part of the physical experience of the infant. Furthermore, as mentioned above, without her (or her facsimile), there is no experience! Mother is an omnipotent, essential, life-giving source to every infant.

> *There was something formless yet complete,*
> *That existed before heaven and earth;*
> *Without sound, without substance,*
> *Dependent on nothing, unchanging,*
> *All pervading, unfailing,*
> *One may think of it as the mother of all things under heaven.*

As we cross the boundaries from the First Quadrant into the Second, we become abruptly aware of something being there with the self: Mother. Even though, as infants, we do not experience Mother as being a separate entity, we do experience a division... a rift. Even the symbol for Cancer is like two entities facing in opposite directions and looks very similar to the Chinese symbol for yin and yang. That pattern is the Oriental symbol for a world of opposites too. As we evaluate the astrological formula that precedes the synthesizing Fourth Archetype, we can see how it systematically carries an affinity with that symbol. We begin with pure creation of male energy (Mars), and ground that with the receptiveness, the seductiveness of femininity (Venus), and then ascertain the concepts (Mercury) of light and dark, black and white.

It's valuable at this point to gain a higher understanding of the concept of 'Antagonism.'

Webster's *New World Dictionary* defines antagonism thusly:

1. *the state of being opposed or hostile to another or to each other; opposition or hostility; 2. an opposing force, principle, etc.; specif., a mutually opposing action that can take place between organisms, muscles, drugs, etc*

The word is almost always used as a reflection of the first half of the definition, as hostility. But consider this: every muscle in the human body without exception has its antagonist. Without it, movement would not be possible. The tension involved in a vibrating violin string is a result of antagonism. It could be argued that all vibration is a result of antagonism. And as we know from physics, manifest form is in a constant state of vibration.

In other words, the antagonisms created by the polarities within the horoscope are necessary and cosmically intentional structures.

Even though it's difficult to tell if the world inherently produced opposites, or if it was our ancestor's perception of the world, generated by our mother who gained her perception from her mother, and so forth (it definitely brings the Chicken and Egg

Question into mind), the world of opposites is logically incorporated within this symbol. Our reality of being born means descending into a world that is full of opposites, and it is definitely Mother who introduces us into this world of dichotomies. When you cried as an infant, and Mother didn't come—it made no difference that she was probably in the bathroom! You were abandoned and in pain. Your world was filled with morbid sensations of horror and death.

For verification, the incorporation of the above into duality can be readily experienced when one brings their particular (biological) mother to mind. Think of your mother, and tell me (even if you've gone through years of therapy to release all the ambiguities) that there are no love/hate dichotomies that flood your mind. Your own childhood memories, your mother's image can readily turn into an all-consuming, energy-depleting demon.

This archetypal image is just as prominent in our psyche as the image of the Madonna. The wicked, devouring mother and the good mother lavishing affection are two sides of the great Mother Goddess who reigns over this psychic stage. Joseph Campbell points out that in pre-Homeric mythology the place of honor was not held by the male god of *"the sunny Olympic pantheon, but by a goddess, darkly ominous...Her consort was typically in serpent form; and her rites were not characterized by the blithe spirit of manly athletic games, humanistic art, social enjoyment, feasting and theater that the modern mind associates with Classical Greece, but were in spirit dark and full of dread."*

Joseph Campbell goes on to describe how the offerings were *"not of cattle, gracefully garlanded"* but were pigs and humans and held in twilight groves and fields where the fresh blood poured into a bottomless abyss. For these rituals were not of a shared feast of giving and receiving, but rather one to *"be rid of"*. He then quotes Jane Ellen Harrison as saying, *"The beings worshipped, were not rational human, law-abiding gods, but vague, irrational, mainly malevolent...spirit-things, ghosts and bogeys and the like, not yet formulated and enclosed into god-head."* Therefore it was the idea *"that if the negative aspect of the daemon was dispelled, health and well-being, fertility and fruit, would issue of themselves from their natural source."*

The insensate life of instincts combines the most meaningless destruction, along with the supreme meaningfulness of creation. This archetype takes into its bosom the alpha and omega of life's experiences. For what resides there, as we leave infancy and make our way through life, are all our memories. The word sub-consciousness, and all its implications, is now the sanctioned, contemporary word for memories, that part of one's self that rules, oftentimes with terror, over every thought and decision we make for all of our lives!

Psychological theory defines the subconscious as the device—the source—that makes us what we are, throughout our lives, each and every day; and the subconscious mind was developed at that time when we cried in our crib, and mother came—or didn't come. What we feel about today was formed in the cradle. All of humans' living can be seen as a pulsation back and forth between the polar movement initiated in our infancy; I need you—I don't need you, hold me—let me go, protect me—release me. In the womb we were attached to mother by the umbilical cord—yet we were separate. After birth we were attached to her by our need for nourishment, containment and protection, yet we were separate. As adults we carry with us, as psychic structures, our internalized picture of mother as the nourishing matrix, yet we are separate. Go too far to one extreme, and you are alone, abandoned. Go too far to the other, and you are smothered: s-MOTHERED. This changeable, sensitive, moody, impressionable quality is well reflected by the Moon.

Our hidden, buried subconscious code of life determines the decisions we make, and then, the subsequent outcome of our life. It is the source, the well-spring that dictates how we accomplish each of our goals. At that time, we made our basic decisions based on our "Right to Life." Consequently, the overwhelming might of the subconscious can be a loving and devoted Mother, or a devouring and destructive Mother—archetypally, the Evil Mother. And it doesn't matter whether she appears as the bloodstained

goddess of death, plague, famine, flood—the force of instinct—
or if she is the sweetness that lures us into our own destruction.
Destruction by any name is still destruction!

On the other hand, those of us who have acquired, through
a healthy childhood or developed through therapy, the good mother
archetype, can own a subconscious of fullness and abundance. The
loving and devoted Mother archetype is the dispenser of life and
happiness, the nutrient earth, the cornucopia of the fruitful womb.
Ideally, The Great Mother is mankind's instinctive experience of
the world's depth and beauty, of the goodness and graciousness of
Mother Nature who daily fulfills the promise of redemption and
resurrection of new life and new birth. Nevertheless, it matters
little which reigns over this domain, the following is quite true.

For what the center brings
Must obviously be
That which remains to the end ...
               (Goethe, Westostlicher Diwan)

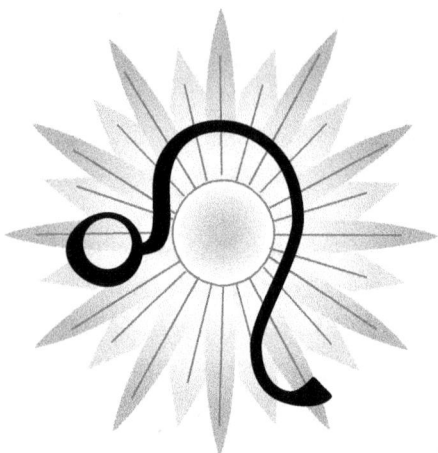

Chapter 8

The Fifth Archetype

Sun~Leo~Fifth House
Fire~Fixed~ Succedent

We have just completed the first course of action into human development. To summarize this matrix, one could say that it is: the encounter of existence and the definition of personal space in the physical body-world; the exposure to, and the discrimination of, the physical body-world; the registering and then rationalizing of one's involvement with the physical body-world (all of which fit quite nicely into the First Quadrant); and finally, the Fourth is the vehicle through which this involvement—this primordial drama—is materialized: the process of physical manifestation.

As mentioned with the First Archetype, this first composite is the contract we sign when we come into this incarnation. "I do solemnly swear that I will spend this lifetime being who I was born to be ..." And once we cross over that threshold and enter unconditionally into the physical body-world, we have to go forward. It's like going into the Marine Corps. We take the orders our "Higher Selves" issued us and go through the training program(s).

Of course, one can get a copy of these orders if one chooses. One of the ways to get a copy is through intensive psychotherapy, but a better way is to understand the pattern of an astrological chart. Nevertheless, if one gets a copy of the orders, it makes the training program(s) easier—like having a map and schedule of events at Disney World when you go there on vacation. In fact, that's a good metaphor for life: one goes on a vacation at Earth-World. The entity comes down to Earth, gets into an Earth Suit, and has a myriad of physical adventures. Each individual ticket determines the kind of rides one goes on in his Earth Suit. It's really just an extravaganza vacation from the real routine of the universe.

At the end of each synthesis, each course of action, we have a merger or an end-product. The end product of this first process is the subconscious mind—that place where the instincts live. This is the place that generates the motivations of our entire lives, the place that "makes us do it"—and often times it can be quite a self-defeating "it."

The Origins and History of Consciousness—a book written by the respected Jungian psychologist, Erich Neumann—is a manual for going into the depths of the Fifth Archetype. Coming from the development of the First Quadrant—and specifically the synthesis of the Fourth Archetype—summing up that experience that launches us into the development of consciousness, or the Fifth, is suitably articulated by Dr. Neumann's words: *"Exposed to the dark forces of the world and the subconscious, early life feeling is necessarily one of constant endangerment. Life in the psychic cosmos of the primitive is a life full of danger and uncertainty...these all-pervading effluences shows itself in fears, emotional outbursts, orgiastic frenzies and psychic epidemics..."*

As we launch into the next process (some fellow Earth adventurers choose not to go beyond the basic training), we begin to ponder the source of our motives. Thus, out of this infantile subconscious, constantly aware of its ties to the matrix from which it sprang, comes an independent system. The fiery beginning of this system—Sun/Leo—is the conscious development of the ego.

Within all mythological accounts of the beginning of our world, heaven and earth are separated and distinguished from one another. In Jungian depth psychology, the ego's archetypal representation is poised between the lower, feminine world of earth and body, and the higher, masculine world of heaven and spirit. And in the astrological paradigm, the Fifth House is poised between the lower part of the chart (*Imum Coeli*, which literally means 'bottom of the sky') and the ascent into light (the Descendant). The 30-degrees of Cancer from the IC to the fifth house cusp marks the innards of the earth. Subsequently, this lower earth-world metaphorically, as well as astrologically, is the Great Mother. This, in turn, makes it hostile to the ego, or the state of consciousness.

On the other hand, the Sixth House is the ascending position of a transiting planet into the light of the horizon—the Descendant. In perfect balance, Virgo, the corresponding sign to the Sixth House, is equidistant on the other side of Leo, subsequently sandwiching the Fifth between the lower earth-world and the descent into light. In this beginning stage, consciousness has not yet developed a firm foothold to withstand the flood of subconscious contributions; it feels itself as a defenseless speck, enveloped and helplessly dependent. Meanwhile, in mythology, heaven, which is illuminated by the Sun, is metaphorically sensed as the ego-friendly world of the spirit and is personified as the benevolent All-Father, disconnecting from the womb and taking a new attitude up to the world.

When considering this all-important Archetype, there is a danger to attributing Ego solely (no pun intended) to the Sun. The Ego is a multiply determined psychological entity, and while its interface with Solar principles is great, it would be a mistake to associate Ego exclusively with the Sun. The ego is often associated with the "self," which is a synthesis of every part of the development of the personality (or chart). Carl Jung calls this part of the "Self" the 'supraordinate personality.' He theorizes that the Self is felt more as an object, than a subject, because of its unconscious component, which can only come to the consciousness indirectly, by way of projection. Therefore the ego is related to the Self as only part of the whole.

So, what one steps into upon entering the Fifth Archetype is the "consciousness" of Self. It is the energy that creates individuality…the center of your beingness…the wellspring of your creativity, self expression, validation, approval, applause, strokes, and so forth. Just as the sun is the center of the solar system, the Fifth is the center of your identity; it is how the Self relates to one's central identification.

The Sun is often said to represent the Heart. The Italian term for Heart is cuore and the French origin for Heart is *coeur.* From those two words we get the English word "core." When you think of someone you know who you would say has a lot of heart, is it the same as saying he/she has a lot of ego? It's close, but it obviously is not the same. Someone with a lot of heart has something of the quality of generosity, of warmth, of centeredness, of self-knowledge. There is a quality of fun and of playfulness there too. And, inevitably, others gravitate to such a person, much like the Sun itself.

What has happened when the organism has reached the stage symbolized by the Fifth Archetype is that it breaks free to an extent. There is a strong amount of integration that has taken place through the first cycle of the four elements. The Fifth enjoys the benefits of whatever integration has occurred. This is the Archetype of recognizing who you are. The Self is formed and conscious and ready for adventure. The ego is its servant who all too often mistakes itself for the master. Recall the statement, *"the ego is related to the Self as only part of the whole."*

Let me preface all of this by pointing out the equal split of this synthesis or process. The Fifth and Sixth Archetypes are clearly in the Second Quadrant; the Seventh and Eighth Archetypes are above the horizon in the Third Quadrant. The Fifth and Sixth are within the Quadrant of differentiation and growth, personal integration—subjective awareness of not-self. From the Fourth Archetypal expression, we begin to reach up and out, with the connection still unsure. Who can be any more obviously insecure than a Leo? It is said that our Sun sign belongs to us only with our maturity. And, maturity can only come to those of us who can see ourselves and accept what we see. This often involves a suppression of ego, as ego pretty much always sees what it wants to see. Again, referring to Erick Neumann, who refers to this phase as that when consciousness begins to turn into self-consciousness, *"that is to recognize and discriminate itself as a separate individual ego..."* It's when *"the maternal uroboros [subconscious development] overshadows it like a dark and tragic fate. Feelings of transitoriness and mortality, impotence and isolation, now color the ego's picture..."*

Neumann goes on to say that the transition into this stage can only be achieved by the strugglers. It is brought about by the fear of the Great Mother's absorption back into the womb—or being the projection through which the mother lives. This turning away from the Great Mother can be seen in the mythological figures of Narcissus, Pentheus, and Hippolytus. All three of these males resist the love of the great goddesses, and the end result appears to be grave punishment. In the case of Narcissus, however, let's look closer. Narcissus, who rejects love, is punished by becoming totally infatuated with the next face he sees. Upon looking into a pool of water, the next face he sees is his own!

This story could be interpreted in a couple of different ways: first, to become conscious of oneself, one must turn away from the alluring promise of feminine absorption; second, if one rejects initial love to look into the pool—the subconscious—to see his own image, he can gain a love of self that otherwise can't be found. It's the tendency of an ego to be conscious of itself, to see itself in a mirror; self-reflection is a necessary characteristic of the pubertal phase of human development. However, persistence in this phase has fatal effects. Neumann tells us that the *"breaking of the Great Mother fixation through self-reflection is not a symbol of autoerotism, but of centroversion."*

The Sun is the central, life-giving force in our solar system, around which everything else orbits. The manner in which it is life-giving, however, is by reflection—direct solar radiation is deadly. Consequently, reflection is the key word here. It's impossible for the Sun to see itself, and the only way it can know its brightness is by seeing its reflection off the other planets. Subsequently, the Sun in our charts is how we get our reflection. And, metaphorically, it sees itself by reflecting off the rest of the planets in the chart. In the physical world, it is how we feel about ourselves after we walk into a room full of people and say hello. The way they respond to us determines how we can feel about ourselves.

And, as referenced above, it is the All-Father. It's the "good father" archetype. The one who tells us he's proud, and that we've performed well. "A chip off the old block" tells the full story of the Fifth Archetype in the father-child inner-relationship.

Of course, if our father ignores us, if he's reading the paper, or watching TV, or, simply ignores our existence, then that reflects—sets—our self-worth, too. This is often the scenario that comes out of many contemporary families. If the Father ignores his children, this results in a personally poor self-image. It gives them the message that they don't exist, that they can't make a positive impact.

Therefore, it is important that children be allowed to be the center of attention, that they be allowed to show off, and that they have a safe space for appropriate resistance to parental dominance. A quote from Neumann, *"persistence in this phase has fatal effects."* is the keystone here. Only with emphasis on this phase of our development can we enable the development of a healthy and integrated inner child within the individuals in our culture. Without this integration, we become obsessed with the process, always hearing the Great Mother's whispers about not being too loud, not wanting too much, not being the center of attention. Without a healthy inner child, we persistently reach for our Sun.

As well, like the mythology suggests, it's romance. It's romance because what we are truly saying when we say we've met someone really wonderful is that we've met someone who reflects us back in the way we like to feel about ourselves. At the time of falling in love, our best selves emerge into awareness. Our perception is heightened. We lose or gain weight—whichever best suits our most perfect self; we are conscious of our physical-ness, whether it is how we dress, or the feelings of our bodies. Leo is the second Fixed sign of the Zodiac. This puts it at a 90°, or Square, angle to Taurus, which is like running a power-line between the two Archetypes, giving them a soul connection. Taurus is the primal sensuality and physical alliance to the corporeal world. At this point, we are presenting our physical-ness to the world for a reflection of our worth.

On the other hand, if we can resist the projection of the Good Father, or the Great Mother onto another, we can delve deeper into our own love of self. Those who have chosen a life of solitude for a certain length of time have found the experience very enlightening, as far as self-discovery is concerned. Those who have chosen to do this have emerged with more wisdom to make a conscious commitment to another, which of course, falls into the Seventh. Perhaps that is the process introduced in the Sixth, so that the asteroid Vesta (for the Vestal Virgins) takes her place as a co-ruler.

Nevertheless, the Fifth is the inner child, and subsequently is the creative force within the human experience. Creativity is a major keyword within this archetype. That's not difficult to understand, because without a healthy child within us, there can be no active imagination, and therefore, no creativity.

Chapter 9

The Goddesses Among Us

An Introduction to the Asteroids & Their Connection to the Sixth and Seventh Archetypes

Whenever there is the discovery of a planet or an additional body inside our solar system, it correlates with the elevation of our thought processes and subsequently raises our consciousness. Therefore, it seems to have an alliance with, as well as to substantiate, Jung's theory of synchronicity and archetypes. The evidence of this is apparent when one evaluates the correlation of a discovered body and its archetypal effects on history. Since events are best assimilated through hindsight, we can readily see the effects Uranus' discovery had on our culture. As this discovery infiltrated our Western System, the results were the revolutionary wars that brought about the elevation of the common people into the social system. Its introduction to our consciousness gave us the idea, and subsequently the ideals, of human rights.

On the other hand, the Vedic (Hindu) astrological system didn't recognize Uranus, and their social system reflects that denial. They maintained a cast system that stymied India's socioeconomic balance. This is an obvious reflection of a social system that has become stalled at Saturn reality. Only within this century have some of the more modern Vedic astrologers begun to place some, or all, of the outer planets into their charts, and the Western world is full of Indians attending our universities!

That indirectly brings me to the asteroids. Anecdotal evidence has suggested that the denial of the discovery of a celestial body and the subsequent adaptation of that denial into our astrological system could be limiting our conscious development. On the other hand, there are equal arguments regarding "too many objects being discovered," and saying that they're just "space junk." There is no denying that the basic ten planets can tell us much; but we must remember that it has only been over the past three centuries that we have gained the outer three planets. Another strong argument for "space junk" is just how junky our Western lifestyle has become. Moreover, with the comprehension of synchronicity, there has been no delay in the interpretation of a new object: it gets a name, and instantly has a dimension. Even if an asteroid is named Sally, there is some story that will create an archetypal "Sally." It takes on a specific meaning when querying a chart about a person named Sally. At this point, that particular asteroid becomes eminently important. Zip Dobyns wrote volumes of material relating to the asteroids and their significance in Mundane charts. Throughout most of her career she published a quarterly newsletter called *Asteroid World* in which there were numbers of cases relating to the coincidental placement of the many bodies in the asteroid belt between Mars and Jupiter.

This material, however, only relates to the first four asteroids discovered that have since been widely considered the most major ones, and are routinely used in charts by many astrologers. They are: Ceres, Pallas, Juno, and Vesta. It should be noted that in 2006, Ceres (the largest of all the asteroids) was elevated to the "dwarf planet" category, to include Pluto and other planets discovered beyond his orbit. It remains common practice, though, among many astrologers who use the asteroids, to continue using Ceres in company with Pallas, Juno and Vesta.

Zip Dobyns and her daughter and colleague, Maritha Pottenger, introduced me to these additional feminine archetypal energies in the early 1980's, and it was then that I gained a richer and more profound understanding of the Sixth and Seventh Archetypes. It's not that Mercury doesn't play an important role in characterizing the sign of Virgo, but rather that Vesta and Ceres take the Sixth Archetype into a three-dimensional depth and compassion that Mercury simply can't offer. In modern astrological rulership (for in traditional astrology, Mercury in Virgo is quite significant) Mercury in Virgo seems to be more solemn and stoic than the mythology portrays. Even early writing by Robert Hand in his 1980's masterpiece, *Horoscope Symbols*, questions Mercury's position here: *"The game-playing aspect of Mercury is missing in Virgo; Virgo is very serious. Mercury has no special concern with duty, while Virgo does."*

This point is not to negate Mercury's position here, but rather stimulate your thinking on this planet-sign partnership. Analytical thinking on this rulership is essential, because in traditional astrology Mercury is not only a ruler in Virgo, it is exalted there as well. Mercury loves the attention to detail implied by this sign. Mercury loves, as well, the mutability. Its the earthiness that can present the challenge. Similar to Mars' exaltation in Capricorn, this exaltation in an Earth sign may not, at first glance, be the most comfortable for the planet involved, but it is the most efficient. The qualities implied by this sign give Mercury exactly what it needs to be most productive. Mercury, the Psycho-pomp, actually gets in and fits in anywhere it wants. The question is: in what sign does Mercury do its best, when the qualities are integrated? Traditional astrology answers this question with: Virgo!

Contemporary astrology, through the 1980s, has Mercury exalted in Aquarius (and there's something to be said about that exaltation, as well). Nonetheless, there is definitely something very Mercurial about the Sixth Archetype. Mercury is known for his cunningness, and what could be more cunning than a Virgo fixing something and not having enough parts! Too, the Sixth's mind is very quick, and it is definitely detail-oriented and geared toward solving problems, all of which could not be attributed to any planet other than Mercury. There is something missing, though. The Sixth is much more caring than Mercury's character seems to be. As well, Mercury's myths do not bend him toward devotion. The statement of value from the ancients is that when Mercury is caring, when Mercury is devoted, when Mercury is compassionate (not unlike when Mars is disciplined and structured), he is at his best.

Anyone experiencing a person with a strong Sixth Archetype influence will relate to what is currently being stated. A Sixth Archetype-type person has a warmth and a compassion that can't be found when one reads the mythological description of Mercury in the Third. There is no doubt that a Virgo can possibly take a problem, project, or issue and be dogged and relentless; that can certainly be a side of Mercury. On the other hand, it could just as easily be the characteristic of a Vestal Virgin.

This is an essential, oft-neglected and frequently trivialized dynamic. This Sixth Archetype is pivotal in importance. Let's review a little. The earth's axial rotation shows us the Sixth House as that place into which the planets, in their apparent motion, set. It is the diurnal entrance into the underworld. At the same time the earth's orbital path, the Sun's apparent position, shows us this place as the threshold into the area south of the celestial equator. For us in the northern hemisphere it marks the end of the growing season and the beginning of the work of harvest. Without good and proper work in this domain, you can forget surviving through the winter. Without good and proper work in this domain, you can forget effective and functional operation of any and all of the last six Archetypal dynamics.

As you will discover later, Virgo, with her sheaf of grain, is a natural partner to both Ceres, Goddess of agriculture, and Vesta,

Goddess of evocative, sacred ritual. For those of you who have not had the pleasure of becoming introduced to the four major asteroids—and even those of you who have—you are about to see how the Sixth (and subsequently the Seventh) are, at least, related to their energy.

The first four asteroids to be discovered were identified between 1801 and 1807—from Ceres, the first, to Vesta, the brightest. These asteroids and their finding marked a predisposition of women in Western history. Until the nineteenth century, women could aspire to be a Mother or a Whore: a Moon Woman, or a Venusian Woman. Even though the Woman's Movement was not truly recognizable until the late 1800s, a few women were already stepping on a few heads to form a pathway. The one who stands out most prominently is Jane Austin (1775-1817). One of Austin's most notable qualities was the fact that she was educated: literate. There is recorded dialogue from that time period, concerning the education of females, which is virtually a carbon copy of the dialogue spoken in the South in the 1950-1960s about integrating education for Black people. Of course, Jane Austin's educated arrogance led her right into becoming the first published woman writer.

With an astrologer's tongue-in-cheek, the eye-catching fact is that, even though she started writing while she was quite young, her works were not actually published until after the discovery of the asteroids. Her first published book, *Sense and Sensibility,* in 1811, remains a classic of the feminine profile.

Simultaneously, women being born during this period would change the face of woman's history—as well as history itself. Within a hundred years, woman's predicament had totally changed. The list of Woman's Who's-Who trails off over the horizon during the nineteenth century. Women took up personal and social causes that had never been conceived of before. And, after they planted the seeds, the twentieth century woman sprang forth and blossomed.

Eleanor Bach was the first person to bring the asteroids into contemporary astrology. She published the first asteroid ephemerides in January 1973, giving their positions every five days. Later Rique Pottenger worked out the formulae of motion and programmed the first daily asteroid ephemeris, *The Asteroid Ephemeris 1883-1999* through TIA Publications in 1977. That book was republished by ACS Publications in 1999. In 2008, Rique Pottenger's updated version, *The Asteroid Ephemeris 1900-2050: Ceres, Pallas, Juno, Vesta, Chiron and Black Moon Lilith,* was published by Starcrafts Publishing, with an introductory article by Zipporah Dobyns, Ph.D.

After asteroid ephemerides were published, and astrologers actually began using these bodies in horoscopes, the most significant changes began occurring among the masses. The mid-1970s truly mark the era when the Women's Liberation Movement became fully apparent. There are more than a few signs of this emergence of new feminine awareness; our entire social structure has transformed. Another factor of obvious magnitude is that concurrent with the women's movement came the emergence of the Gay Liberation Movement. People from all walks of life are overtly acknowledging deep and urgent forces within themselves. Because of this rebirth of the goddess into women, it has brought a significant impact into the lives of men, too.

As women began to change, the conventional male behavior was no longer acceptable; it became impossible for men to relate to women in traditional ways. Until this time, it was perfectly acceptable for men to project their Moon and Venus onto a woman. Home and nurturing was the woman's domain, and men felt awkward when faced with the possibility of performing any task that was considered feminine. The family's base survival—food preparation, cleaning, and children—was woman's work, and men were supposed to go keep themselves occupied some place else. A woman's breasts either had a kid hanging off them, or, a Merry Widow pushing them up, to reveal a male-satisfying cleavage. Either way, her sole purpose was to fulfill whatever particular image the male in her life needed.

Men, therefore, have been forced to acquire a completely different attitude around their roles and projected expectations;

however, this has enabled them to explore a new dimension of their own psyches. Men are now permitted to cry, feel sad and depressed, have weaknesses and doubts, and as well, feel the joy of intimacy—with his children and his mate. He is no longer locked out of his own emotional life, nor the emotional lives of others. As well, there is no longer the division between woman's work and man's work. Women have permeated occupational areas that were traditionally male, and men have gone into occupations that have been regarded as feminine—nurses, flight attendants, telephone operators, secretaries—even some nannies. As well, the responsibilities of daily maintenance—cooking, dishwashing, bathroom cleaning, laundry, etc.—are now preformed jointly in most homes where both of the mates are employed, or have careers. The housewife is a dying reference.

One of the most prominent changes, though, that has occurred is within the male parenting role. Until the 1970s, men took no active role in child birthing. They were banished to another part of the house or yard, if the child were born at home, or to a waiting room when hospital deliveries began. Now, men go to child-birthing training classes with their wives, so that they can help facilitate their child's delivery. In the ensuing period, we have seen them take a more prominent and active role in the raising of their very young children. With the women sharing in the financial support of the family, men are expected to get up at night and participate in child-care maintenance. What this has done for men is to integrate the ability to care for and nurture into their consciousness.

Simultaneously, women have been creating a deeper desire for the men in their lives to inter-relate in a more sensitive, emotional, and nurturing way. The tall, silent type of male, who doesn't show his pain—emotionally or physically—and leaves the woman to surmise what is transpiring within his inner-self, no longer holds the mystique that it did in past generations. John Wayne is no longer the icon to the New Woman that he was to women earlier this century.

Chapter *10*

The Sixth Archetype
Mercury (Ceres and Vesta)-Virgo
Sixth House
Earth- Mutable- Cadent

The Sixth Archetype is one of the most misunderstood parts of the zodiacal structure; however, if one follows the astrological paradigm that whatever Fire creates, Earth brings into materialization, then it is easily understood. If the Fifth Archetype is ego development, then the materialization of ego development would be self-worth. The fledgling ego flies into the Sixth to accomplish its realization. This is the area where we set forth to manifest our creations into physical reality—the author wants to write the book, the architect wants to build the building, the producer wants to see the product. The Sixth is the archetype of self-fulfillment. Consequently it would, by its very nature, be associated with production.

Now, if one doesn't feel productive, one really doesn't feel good, not only emotionally, but physically as well. One must feel as if counted upon (productive), within the world to feel whole. If one does not—if an individual doesn't feel fulfilled—then he or she doesn't feel at ease. When an individual doesn't feel at ease, the result is dis-ease (disease).

What we have here is all of the First Quadrant, as it is synthesized into the Fourth Archetype. At that point, the Fifth is born from that fertile womb, and stands up on its wobbly legs in the Sixth. The Sixth House is the house where a transiting planet is preparing (remember, the planets transit through the houses counter-clockwise) to go above the horizon.

Metaphorically, the Sixth Archetype is the preparation of everything that you have become since birth emerging into the light. When we become healthy, conscious beings, we take our awareness into productivity. On the other hand, if our development is contaminated emotional rubbish, then we become unhealthy.

If we focus on the Descendant, then view the Fire-Earth-Air-Water 120-degree arc surrounding it (Archetypes 5, 6, 7 and 8), it's easy to see how this can be viewed as the social element grouping. It is obvious too, that this second element grouping comes between the first and the third element quartet, between the personal and the collective set. Seen in this context, this particular 5-6-7-8 rhythm could be said to be Courtship, Apprenticeship, Relationship, and Fusion. Or it could be Play, Work, Partnership, and Sex (Intimacy). You can sense, as well, the rhythm of Yang-Yin-Yang-Yin at play here. How about saying Self-Realization, Self-Fulfillment, Self-Other Balance, and Self-Yielded Merging. It's important to get a feeling for this rhythm of these four to understand how this dynamic functions and too, exactly how this all-important Sixth Archetype fits in.

When we remember that the fountainhead of our consciousness is the subconscious, we can begin to work at the source of what is being manifested in the Sixth—that which precedes disease. There is a book written by Louise Hay that is a handholding, step-by-step guide into our beliefs that are stuck in the subconscious, and subsequently are the directives that block the adequate advent of a healthy body and life. She believes that our body is a mirror of our inner thoughts and beliefs, and subsequently we create illness in our bodies. She claims, *"Every cell within your body responds to every single thought you think and every word you speak."* This theory has recently been scientifically substantiated by noted biologist Bruce Lipton in his book *The Biology of Belief.*

At this point, one can correlate a dual rulership of Mercury. Within the Third Archetype, we saw how one determines reality through their perceptions; in the Sixth Archetype, one manifests their perceptions into productivity – or action. It can be where we actually bring our thoughts into physical manifestation. It is where we're productive, or where we're frustrated.

Since we are the only person who thinks with our mind, we are the orchestrator of our reality, or manifestations. Subsequently, the Sixth generates the ability to rejoice in accomplishments— one's own accomplishments and the accomplishments of others around them, on the one hand. On the other hand, it can produce a critical, judgmental attitude toward one's own abilities, along with the abilities of others. When one is unsure of oneself and distrusts his accomplishments, oftentimes he will project those inadequacies onto others. This particular Virgoan quality is known as nit-picking.

Summing up the Sixth Archetype at its most simplistic, let's look at it this way; "T minus two minutes and counting..." such as what goes on just before take-off. The entire crew is going through the checklist, detail by detail, to make sure everything is functional and working. This is an active and necessary process of seeking out the non-functional for immediate repair. The process is essential and the analogy is most appropriate. We're on Earth, just about to take off above the horizon into Air. Systems need to be in working order for the flight. There is great risk involved. In the flight, there's an inherent risk of crashing and burning. For Self, we're just about to truly encounter The Other, also no easy task. This is the dynamic of preparing for our flight. As with any and all of these functions, they have their place, and they can and will be exaggerated and misused. Inappropriate nit-picking is one such misuse.

Looking at this in another way, using the chart as a metaphor for a 24-hour day, the Sixth House is specifically the time of twilight. As the earth turns within the day, the Sixth House is metaphorically the space that is immediately after sunset. During this time of day, there's not enough light to clearly see, but it is not quite totally dark. In the chronological structure of the horoscope, we are coming around from the IC towards the descendant. Again, we are beginning to come into the light. These observations indicate an area of transformation. This particular transformation is not within the same context as the Eighth Archetype, but rather a transition of light. With the clockwise motion of a 24-hour day, it is a time of decline and rest; within the counter-clockwise motion it is an emergence, an indication of a seed becoming a plant.

Viewed from the perspective of its position between the Yang Archetypes of Five and Seven, the Sixth Archetype can be seen as an area of strong repair and maintenance. Between Self-expression (Fifth) and Relationship (Seventh) come hard work and the rituals of craftsmanship (Sixth). This is where we polish our act and get down to the nitty-gritty details before encountering the Other at the Descendant. And unless we have done that necessary work, we are completely unprepared to deal with others, certainly not in any type of close and/or intimate relationship.

Chapter 11

A Closer Look at Ceres

Ceres, like the sign of Virgo, has a many faceted image. Her mythological story breathes life into the Sixth Archetype. Ceres' image and the image of her maiden daughter are the perfect personification of the Virgo/Pisces polarity. The many facets and dimensions of Virgo are totally reflected in her life.

In the original Greek myth, Ceres' name is Demeter, which translates into *da mater* and means earth mother. The harvest time that embraces the time of Virgo reminds us of the earth's bounty, and how, without her yield, we could not live. By definition, the Virgo Mother differs from the Moon Mother. The Moon Mother is the Mother Archetype; the Moon Mother is the one that gives birth. On the other hand, the Virgo Mother regenerates life—reconstructs, reconditions and rebuilds. She was the mother who provided and supplied, as opposed to the Great Mother, who protected, enveloped and/or consumed.

In the opening of Ceres' story, Jupiter (or Zeus), her brother, freed her after his battle with Saturn and the Titans. She eventually lived among the mortals, giving humanity grain. Subsequently, she is the Goddess of agriculture and of the harvest. One of her most prestigious functions in the mythological-archetypal structure, however, was that of the devoted mother of Proserpina (called Kore/Persephone in the earlier Greek version of the myth), and the subsequent account of the abduction and rape of her daughter. When the story commences, Mother and daughter are together and happy, and Ceres gifts the earth with a perpetual season of harvest. The world knew no deprivation, no winter. Ceres/Demeter was also known for her great beauty, and Proserpina/Persephone was just as beautiful as her mother. Subsequently, men and gods alike desired this fair, young maiden. Nonetheless, the love between mother and daughter outweighed the efforts of any suitors.

The beginning of the Homeric *Hymn To Demeter* tells of Persephone's abduction by Hades (Pluto):

(ll. 1-3)I begin to sing of rich-haired Demeter, awful goddess -- of her and her trim-ankled daughter [Persephone] *whom* [Hades] *rapt away, given to him by all-seeing Zeus the loud-thunderer.*

(ll. 4-18) Apart from Demeter, lady of the golden sword and glorious fruits, she [Persephone] *was playing with the deep-bosomed daughters of Oceanus and gathering flowers over a soft meadow, roses and crocuses and beautiful violets, irises also and hyacinths and the narcissus, which Earth made to grow at the will of Zeus and to please the Host of Many, to be a snare for the bloom-like girl—a marvellous, radiant flower. It was a thing of awe whether for deathless gods or mortal men to see: from its root grew a hundred blooms and it smelled most sweetly, so that all wide heaven above and the whole earth and the sea's salt swell laughed for*

joy. And the girl was amazed and reached out with both hands to take the lovely toy; but the wide-pathed earth yawned there in the plain of Nysa, and the lord, Host of Many, [Hades] *with his immortal horses sprang out upon her -- the Son of Cronos, He who has many names.*

(ll. 19-32) He caught her up reluctant on his golden car and bare her away lamenting. Then she cried out shrilly with her voice, calling upon her father, the Son of Cronos [Zeus, also a son of Cronos], *who is most high and excellent. But no one, either of the deathless gods or of mortal men, heard her voice, nor yet the olive-trees bearing rich fruit: only tender-hearted Hecate, bright-coiffed, the daughter of Persaeus, heard the girl from her cave, and the lord Helios, Hyperion's bright son, as she cried to her father, the Son of Cronos. But he was sitting aloof, apart from the gods, in his temple where many pray, and receiving sweet offerings from mortal men. So he, that Son of Cronos, of many names, who is Ruler of Many and Host of Many, was bearing her away by leave of Zeus on his immortal chariot -- his own brother's child and all unwilling.*

The crone goddess, Hecate and the sun god, Helios, were the only ones who heard her screams, and even though they knew of the scheme, Hecate told Demeter to go to the seer Helios. (She must seek consciousness—the Sun's Archetype.)

When Demeter learned of the abduction from Helios and that the deed was done with the approval of her brother Zeus, she was furious! She realized his intention was for her beautiful daughter to become Queen of the Underworld. Enraged, broken-hearted, and betrayed (feelings that most Virgos can identify with), Demeter wandered about the earth in search of her daughter. Confused with rage, she first took refuge in a town called Eleusis, in the guise of an old woman. There she was welcomed into the house of King Celeus, and in return for the kindness, she taught the art of agriculture to the Eleusinians, which promised a happy life here on earth. Within this part of the myth, she also cared for the royal infant Demophoon, which associates her with day-care and nannying.

After that phase, she retired to her temple. Still broken-hearted and in a rage, she had had enough. Without agreement from Zeus to return Persephone, she made the land infertile as a last resort. Zeus feared all of humanity would die, and there would be no worshipers for the gods and goddesses. He relented and told Demeter that her daughter could return to her, unconditionally, if she had not eaten while in the underworld. If she had eaten (taken in carnal knowledge), then that would be taken into consideration. When Persephone heard his decree, she looked quickly around where she stood and saw a pomegranate laying in the corner. She quickly picked up the fruit consuming six (some say only four) seeds. The multitude of seeds that make up a pomegranate symbolize sperm and eating those seeds means, metaphorically, sexual consummation.

Zeus decreed that since she had eaten the pomegranate seeds, she must share her time between her mother in the outer world and as the Queen of the Underworld. She rejoins Demeter for six months of each year. Demeter rejoices her daughter's return, and weeps when she departs.

Of course, there are other considerations to ponder here within this one account. The most obvious being that she chooses womanhood over maidenhood; she prefers to be a peer to her mother and give up her role as the dependent child.

As the Sun enters Virgo, its magnitude in the northern hemisphere is coming to an end; the approaching journey into the southern hemisphere is imminent—the Underworld to those of us living in the northern hemisphere! And with the encroaching winter come the cold rains of Ceres' (Demeter's) tears.

While Demeter was in Eleusis, a temple was built there to honor her, and she established the sacred mysteries. The

Eleusinian Mysteries go back to a very early period, about 2000 BCE, probably pre-dating the arrival of the Greek settlers. The mysteries represented the deepest religious experience to the ancients and were the only means to divest death of its terror. The sacred drama, which is mostly lost to modern understanding, was the reenactment of the abduction of Persephone and her mother's sorrowfulness. It was fundamentally a "vegetation" rite. It was celebrated at the onset of spring and the onset of autumn up to AD 400.

In his works *Essays on a Science of Mythology*, Carl Jung says of Ceres *"To enter into the figure of Ceres means to be pursued, to be robbed, to be raped, to fail to understand, to rage and grieve, but then to get everything back and be born again."*

Subsequently, we can find an active Ceres in a multitude of functions in our lives and horoscopes. She can introduce lessons of attachment and separation, of sharing and then of letting go. This also associates her with interactions around one's grown children, especially daughters. She is related to food complexes, such as anorexia. She depicts the ability and capacity to work, and of course, she is related to productivity. She not only can be analogous to service, but she also symbolizes concern for workers and/or social service organizations. Ceres halted all production of the land, hence she rules strikes and other expressions of the refusal to work (i.e., Labor Unions).

Chapter *12*

Vesta's Connection to the Sixth Archetype

Vesta, the Roman counterpart to Hestia, was the first Olympian of the twelve Olympian deities to be born to Kronus (Saturn) and Rhea. The first born of the pantheon was sacred and most precious to the Greek's mundane life: the fire in the hearth. Subsequently, hearth and home were synonymous. In Rome, she was worshipped within each household, and her worship lasted until the fourth century of the Christian Era. Since she was the first born, Hestia was the last one to be born from Saturn's stomach when Zeus (Jupiter) freed his siblings; she was offered the first and last libations at sacrificial meals.

Hestia was not merely the goddess of family life, but also of the state, since the city was viewed as a collection of family units. Thus, just as the fire of Hestia was always kept burning in the home, so the prytaneum, or meeting place of the magistrates, was regarded as her special sanctuary. There, a common fire for the public was maintained, and it was from this place that colonists took fire for the public hearth of a new colony.

She was romantically pursued by both Apollo (the Sun god, depicting consciousness) and Poseidon (or Neptune, the modern ruler of Pisces, and the Sixth's polarity); however, she remained a virgin goddess. It is important to know that the word, virgin, in the ancient world, simply meant unmarried. Chastity as a component of virginity is largely an overlaid patriarchal value. Virgin goddesses only indicated that the goddesses embodied the masculine and feminine attributes in their archetypal character.

In Rome, however, Vesta was a public shrine that stood in the Forum, and the priestesses – the Vestal Virgins —tended her fire. The Vestals, four (later six) in number, were selected between the ages of six and ten and served for thirty years. After their service was fulfilled, they could return to private life and could choose to marry; however, if a Vestal in service was found guilty of unchastity, the punishment was to be buried alive. As well, if a Vestal, through negligence, allowed the sacred fire to go out, the punishment was flogging. This image became the archetype of the modern nun.

Nevertheless, the pre-Hellenistic origins of this archetypal energy were somewhat different. In the ancient world, the Great Mother Goddess was the chief deity. This matriarchal society worshipped the metaphorical feminine form of the Moon, and likewise, was served by women. These priestesses were the vestals of the Goddess, and fostered the fertilizing power of the Moon. When they fulfilled their fruitful service, they bore the sons of the royal line. These offspring were known as the Sons of God. This, therefore, is the metaphorical indication of the fertile development of consciousness. All the same, these women were known as virgins, not because they were chaste, but because they were unmarried and belonged to no man. Thus, the virgins of that place in history existed as whole and complete entities unto themselves.

Demetra George wrote an excellent book on the asteroids in the late 1980's named *Asteroid Goddesses* and went into beautiful detail on these major four. She tells that Vesta's *"name is derived from the Sanskrit root vas, meaning 'shining.'"* This asteroid is composed of a particular type of volcanic rock which reflects an extraordinary amount of sunlight making her the brightest rock in the group. Demetra goes on to point out that *"Vesta is symbolized by the Virgin who appears in the Virgo pictograph..."* de facto making this asteroid akin to the Sixth. Moreover, the healthy archetypal expression of the Sixth is the ability to be focused and/or be dedicated, as well as to achieve the ability to psychologically integrate the masculine and feminine within oneself. These characteristics do fit Vesta quite nicely.

Subsequently, Vesta rules both physical and devotional disciplines. Additionally, we can see sexual repression, or its ancient extreme—sexual promiscuity—in this archetype. The positive or negative determination of the latter is how well the individual can integrate the energy into a wholeness of being.

Chapter 13

The Seventh Archetype

Venus (Pallas Athena and Juno)-Libra
Seventh House
Air - Cardinal- Angular

As the Sun treks back over the Equator after completing its mighty presence in the chart's Northern Hemisphere, it creates a precise timing that begins the sign of Libra. When the seasonal Sun goes over the Equator at the Vernal Equinox, it comes into the earth's northern hemisphere; but in the horoscope, it is traveling below the Horizon as it goes into the First House. As the Sun travels over the Equator at the Autumnal Equinox and into the earth's southern hemisphere, it is going into the Seventh House and above the Horizon. With the onset of Aries in the spring, the Sun is moving into the horoscope's realm of the self, or Subjectivity; while in the autumn, the Sun is traveling away from the self into Objectivity. Total polarities—both equally powerful.

A planet positioned above the Horizon in the Seventh House in a chart is as significant as a planet in the First House. The main difference is that the planet in the Seventh House can be projected (or as Zip Dobyns use to say, "You have someone else do it for you."), while in the First House, you can use the energy as a spear as you project yourself out into the world. Nonetheless, both planets are yours, and you manipulate them and use them equally.

A transiting planet—or a planet of prediction (by Transit, Progression, or Solar Arc Direction)—becomes very powerful when it comes above the Horizon and into the Seventh House. With transiting planets, the angles are hallmarks in these cycles, but it also means that after a journey through the Realm of the Subjective, the planet has surfaced into the light for a full evaluation of its recent journey. With Progressions, et al, it is quite significant when a planet goes above the Horizon, because most likely the planet was in the Northern Hemisphere when the individual was born. This individual will probably become more aware of the energy of this planet now, and it will be more accessible in one's consciousness.

The Seventh is the first place where we can see. It is a place where I can see you and you can see me. It is as if we have spent our entire childhood in a dark cave, and we now emerge into the sunlight, seeing each other with blinking eyes. Our awareness is suddenly flooded with the questions, "Who are you? Are we the same, or are you different than me?"

Even though the Seventh is a mediator, it holds the ability to be detached and emotionally non-judgmental. Its intent is that of equality—fairness. Furthermore, just like its opposite — Aries, it's a cardinal point, an angle, and its significance is eminent. One might get away with calling Mutable Air flighty, but this is Cardinal Air. It is not weak. Words like wishy-washy are often used to reflect this archetype; would Cardinal anything be wishy-washy? Not likely! Was Henry Kissinger wishy-washy? Kissinger is the personification of Libra and the Seventh House.

The four asteroids most commonly used in an astrological

chart were introduced in Chapters 9 and 10. It was said that the two asteroids that relate significantly to the Sixth bring a deeper, richer dimension to its meaning and interpretation, and this is even more pronounced with the Seventh Archetype. There have been convincing arguments that Ceres is a co-ruler of the Fourth, but no one can deny how appropriately the mythological stories of Pallas Athena and Juno speak of the archetypal energy of the Seventh. As well, Mercury is seen brilliantly in the Sixth, while the major correlation of Venus that adequately explains her association with the Seventh is affaire d'amour with Mars and other warrior types. That association can just as easily be Venus' rulership of Mars' next-door neighbor, as that of his polarity. The Taurean Venus is more in keeping with a goddess who reveled in carnal pleasure. Venus was not readily known as a mediator; however, Pallas Athena was.

Chapter *14*

Pallas Athena
& The Seventh Archetype

Pallas Athena makes an excellent polarity for Ares/Mars. Remember that a polarity is not totally different energy, but is instead the same energy acted out in opposite ways. She is the most masculine of all the goddesses, and yet still maintains the depth of her femininity. Pallas Athena was the patroness of numerous Greek cities, but her city was Athens. According to legend, in the time of Cecrops, Poseidon and Athena each desired possession of the city. It was to be awarded to the deity who offered the city the most useful gift. Poseidon gave the horse, but Athena planted the olive tree. The city was awarded to her and was named Athens.

As protectress of all cities, Athena was, by necessity, a goddess of warfare. She was, however, supportive of civilized warfare as opposed to mere blood-lust, as is represented by her polarity, Ares/Mars. She was also goddess of skilled and peaceful

pursuits in general, and in particular, the female arts and industries
of spinning and weaving. Too, she contributed to musical arts
by inventing the flute. As Athena Ergane (work-woman), she is
depicted in female attire; but more commonly, she is dressed in
full armor. The little owl (an icon for wisdom), Athene noctua,
was sacred to her, and she is often seen with one riding on her
shoulder.

Her birth was a bit unusual. The Homeric Hymn to Pallas
Athena:

> *"I begin to sing of Pallas Athene, the glorious goddess,
> bright-eyed, inventive, unbending of heart, pure virgin,
> saviour of cities, courageous, Tritogeneia. From his awful
> head wise Zeus himself bare her arrayed in warlike arms
> of flashing gold, and awe seized all the gods as they gazed.
> But Athena sprang quickly from the immortal head and
> stood before Zeus who holds the aegis, shaking a sharp
> spear: great Olympus began to reel horribly at the might
> of the bright-eyed goddess, and earth round about cried
> fearfully, and the sea was moved and tossed with dark
> waves, while foam burst forth suddenly: the bright Son
> of Hyperion stopped his swift-footed horses a long while,
> until the maiden Pallas Athene had stripped the heavenly
> armour from her immortal shoulders. And wise Zeus was
> glad.*
>
> *And so hail to you, daughter of Zeus who holds the aegis!
> Now I will remember you and another song as well."*

The archetypal manifestation is portrayed in the myth. She came
from masculine (Sun) consciousness (and of course, the Seventh
is the Air process of conscious-self development), but even though
she was from the younger generation of the Pantheon, she still
had her origin in the matriarchy. Earlier she was seen as the three
faces of the Libyan snake goddess, Neith—as Pallas, Athene, and
Medusa. This is interesting, since Medusa became the gorgon due
to her anger from being traumatically raped and is often seen as

one of the icons of the Eighth. Her plight was to turn into stone any man who looked upon her face… an interesting image of the Eighth's response to abuse!

Nevertheless, by the time of Greek culture, the three had split into separate entities, and Pallas Athena had become a symbol of the new patriarchal order. She is even portrayed as assisting in the destruction of her matriarchal antecedents —Pallas Athena was instrumental in Perseus' killing of the Medusa, by giving him her shield so he wouldn't need to look directly into her face to inflict the fatal blow. The final blow to women, however, came with Athena's critical participation in the Trial of Orestes.

Orestes was accused of matricide. Of course, like all Greek stories, the entire story is very convoluted. It takes place around the Trojan Wars. Clytemnestra, his mother, was sister to Helen, whose infidelity with a Trojan prince started the war. The story twists and turns, and after Orestes' mother exiled him—so that he could not defend his father, Agamemnon, king of Argos— she killed her husband, his father. The god Apollo (consciousness) commanded that he return and avenge his father's death. The ancient law decreed that killing someone who had no blood relationship was not a crime; however, murdering someone in kinship by blood was forbidden. Therefore avenging his father would require him to kill his mother. A son killing his mother would be considered an "ultimate crime."

After Orestes finalized the deed, he was guilty of a crime against what was considered natural law, and even though it was sanctioned by Apollo, he was pursued by the Erinyes who are above the laws of the gods, and it's their essential purpose to hound the guilt-ridden mind into madness. Subsequently he sought sanctuary at Apollo's alter. There, Pallas Athena intervenes and brings in eleven Athenians to join her in forming a jury to judge Orestes. Apollo acts as the advocate for Orestes, while the Erinyes plead the case for dead Clytemnestra. During the trial, Apollo convinces Athena that, in all marriages, the man is more important than the woman, by pointing out that Athena was born only of Zeus, without a mother. Pallas Athena votes last and casts the final vote for acquittal, thus acquitting Orestes of his crime. She then persuades the Erinyes to accept the verdict, and they eventually did submit.

Although this reduced woman into servitude, even within the role of Mother, her mythological metaphor also put her into a peer position with men. Since she was born from Zeus' head, she was Wisdom personified, and from this position she gave women dignity. Within her mythology she was sought for her judiciousness; she was a wise judge, and is often accredited with many kind attributes that are considered moral and righteous.

Pallas Athena symbolizes creative intelligence, the ability to negotiate, political arts, and androgynous magnetism, and is an indicator of wisdom and intelligence within a chart. Pallas Athena indicates equality among the sexes and generates platonic friendships. The Athena woman sees herself as equal in a Man's world: The Corporate Woman. Overall, Pallas Athena shows an affinity toward "being civilized" and diplomatic.

The core archetypal energy of the Seventh is the art of diplomacy. But diplomacy is not the gentle art one thinks of when they hear the word. It requires that one make assessments of other's motives and intentions. One can't make an error of judgment when dealing with another. One must stay cool in the face of extreme adversity; becoming defensive is not in one's best interest when they are attempting to gain control of a situation. The Seventh rules lawyers, open enemies, conflicts, and debates… and all one-to-one relationships.

As mentioned above, Venus co-rules this area—also ruling Taurus. Even though she can be readily extracted to meet the needs of the sensuous and security-oriented Taurus, when she enters the rulership of Libra, she loses much of her significance and strength in the modern astrologer's mind; in some ways the modern astrologer has turned her into a love-struck, giggling school-girl. The original archetypal Venus—by whichever locales' name— was a goddess to be reckoned with. She definitely was a female who knew her own mind.

The Seventh is the part of ourselves that can make

assessments. And to confuse the Seventh's Venus with giggling love is a gross misconception; she is the icon for the cool-eyed business of relationships and commitments. Having love as criteria for commitment decisions is a relatively new concept. Instead, love and romance are the needs that must be met in the Fifth—the onset of this particular process. The Air conceptualizes (unemotionally) what Fire creates. For eons, and still today in many countries, commitments are made with prudent minds; anyone emotionally involved is removed from the resolution. Equally, the Seventh House is looked upon for business partnerships, as well as marriages.

The previous Air archetype was Gemini. It collected data and created a personal reality. This second Air archetype does no less. With the former, however, one is correlating mundane data; with the latter, one is supposing another's motives. Our minds oftentimes suggest that our reality of the Other is precisely who and what they are. Just like in the Third, we are creating, in our minds, a reality. We are dealing with our own variation of reason with this Archetype, in the same manner as the Third. And this reasoning is personal. It is based on the internal process of the First and Second Quadrants—the Subjective Northern Hemisphere.

Liz Greene points out in that we often poke fun at the distorted visions of life, reality and relationships that others may perceive; but *"not funny when we have to question the very ground upon which we stand ourselves."* Our concepts of others are personal; what is happening in the Seventh is our energy, based on the thought formation of our reality.

What we do here, in this place that is the polarity of the First, is to project upon The Other what, instead, belongs to us. The First is war, but the Seventh is with whom we war. It is the area of open conflict. Here is where we fight with our inner-selves, who are disguised as another person.

But the Seventh is not only where we can openly conflict, but also where we can gain objective understanding through psycho-counseling. Deep analysis belongs to the Eighth; but talk-therapy, that reasons an understanding within relationships, fits squarely into the Seventh. The latter is what is paramount within our culture today and it has become a large industry. The marriage structure is transitioning; but as well, our marriages are ironically like the mythological tales of Hera (Greek) or Juno (Roman) and Zeus (Greek) or Jupiter (Roman).

Chapter 15
Juno, the Seventh Archetype & The Six Polarities

In the more traditional accounts of the Greco-Roman culture, Hera/Juno and her husband, Jupiter/Zeus, formed the archetypal nucleus of the stereotypical dysfunctional family. Jupiter would punish Juno by angrily hurling thunderbolts at her; she would retaliate by working to defeat and humiliate Jupiter, preferably in public. It was even reflected in the myths of their offspring: they were the stereotypical children of a dysfunctional home.

We already know, from her introduction in the chapter on the First Archetype, that Juno doted on her son, Mars. In today's psychology, it would be noted that Juno made Mars her surrogate mate. It's easy to see why the Greek version of this Archetype—Ares—leaned so heavily toward cruelty when you realize the possible projections of his mother, who was definitely malcontented with her husband's promiscuousness and abuse. Her neediness and intimate secrets (possibly about Jupiter's sexual escapades, or their own dysfunctional sexual performances) would have been too much for a young boy's mind to absorb in a healthy manner. With Zeus as the same-sex parent, these projections lead the child to feel his gender and their needs are unacceptable.

Hephaestus (Hephaistos) was their first child, though. His character was typical of the first-born position. He was an overachiever, who had little self-confidence. He possibly labored harder than anyone else in the Pantheon. He was their blacksmith and forged many and various items for his fellow gods and goddesses. In keeping with the character of his birth-station, he was a kind and gentle man; however, he was a disgrace to his divine parents. He was physically deformed, and the fact that he lacked absolute perfection embarrassed them. He was at best abused; at worst, he was ignored.

He was also Venus' marriage partner. She too perpetually humiliated him by being sexually promiscuous with anyone who momentarily caught her fancy; but above all, the greatest humiliation was the public affair she had with his brother, Mars, a coupling that brought about a number of notorious offspring.

The affair Venus had with Mars was a major focus on Mount Olympus. There are possibly more stories about Venus and Mars than any other two of the pantheon. Nonetheless, Juno couldn't go about her life without this relationship affecting her. One could possibly suspect that Venus was Juno's Shadow. Juno is often seen in mythology as consistently jealous and ill-tempered. The problem would be obvious to the most casual mental health therapists, because Venus represents the very principle of promiscuity that Juno hates in Jupiter. Moreover, since Venus is another female, it's harder for Juno to accept. Juno's righteous rage over Venus' infidelity was equally matched by Venus' contempt for monogamous marriage and 'social propriety'.

Can't you just see a family Sunday dinner at Juno's house? Haven't you actually been to one?

Within the study of this zodiacal mandala that dissects each individual field of energy, there is yet another important consideration. The study of the archetypes is incomplete without taking it to the next step, into the polarities, and we are at the point in our studies where it becomes essential to begin this observation.

That is because there are actually not twelve signs, but instead six polarities. The polarities are very important to comprehend, because if one has a firm understanding of them, it is much easier to keep the definitions clear and precise —and to ultimately turn these into delineations.

It is important to stress that a polarity is the same energy, operating at opposite ends of the spectrum. In other words, a single polarity is not two energies that are totally different, such as apples and mountains. A polarity is the same thing, such as the polarity of electricity; however, saying positive and negative–as is used in describing electricity–is a misnomer in astrology. Immediately, the polarity of a positive sign is another positive sign, and the polarity of a negative sign is another negative sign (i.e., Fire is polarized with Air–both positive signs–and Earth is polarized with Water, which are both negative). After the separation between electricity and astrological archetypes is made, however, I'd like to refer to them as masculine —aggressive and/or spiritual (ethereal) —and feminine — receptive and/or soulful (earthy).

It is also important to note that one of each of the pair of polarities is in the Northern Hemisphere, while the other is in the Southern Hemisphere. This clearly indicates that one side is in the subjective mode, while the other is in the objective mode. Many astrologers call the Northern Hemisphere's signs lower, while the Southern Hemisphere holds the higher modes of operation. Again, comparable to the words positive and negative, this connotation lacks clarity.

A better understanding of this would be to look at what these Hemispheres mean. The Northern signs would indicate that these signs are personal in nature; while the Southern Hemisphere's signs would take the polarized energy out into the world–into the land of the Other, so that it is operating in a collective. Higher and lower tend to sound like judgments that cannot apply here. It is just as necessary to develop harmony within our inner selves, as it is to function appropriately with others. As indicated in the concept of polarity, both ends of the spectrum are necessary to activate a functional circuit of energy, if it is to function appropriately with others.

What will be given here are only a few key characteristics based on what you have already learned in your study of the first six Archetypes. This should be enough to stimulate your exploration of the polarities. Of course, your study has demonstrated that we're always speaking of archetypes, and not of characteristics of individual people. Nor, is this examination offered to circumvent your personal contemplation and ultimate understanding. Just remember this very important actuality: the paradigm must fit together. There cannot be something that operates as if it is both below and above the horizon, nor can archetypal energies bleed into one another. If you keep that in the forefront of your mind, you can easily begin to see the polarities and how they function as a whole.

In addition, when you see the whole energy, you can begin to work more efficiently with your own energy, realizing the whole of the polarized energy with which you are currently working. It can even be said that the Archetypal Taurus, for example, implies and has inherent within it, Archetypal Scorpio. Jung called this *"enantiodromia,"* meaning the tendency of things to contain, or become, their opposite. That which is part of you, which is opposite to that with which you can identify, or feel, is exactly that which you project out onto your environment or onto others. To look at both sides of projection, find that particular polarity, then work with it as a whole. This process will bring your life into balance. Oppositions and even squares (since each square is two sets of polarities within the same modality) are subsequently easier to get a handle on, which can then enable you to smooth out and understand these energies.

Utilizing this, let's begin conceptualizing the First Polarity: the Seventh in opposition to the First. This polarity is so obvious that it's hard to bring words into play. The self-centeredness of the First—the impulsiveness, the naiveté, the aggressiveness, and assertiveness—is counterbalanced by the nature of the Seventh's diplomacy and need for harmony. It can, however, be expressed with a bit more simplicity by saying "I'm going to do what I want to do" [Aries], or "I'm going to do what I want to do, diplomatically and with you thinking I'm doing what you want me to do" [Libra].

The First is blunt, saying exactly what he wants to say; the Seventh is euphemistic, saying what he wants to say tactfully and diplomatically. They are both doing exactly the same thing, only at opposite ends of the spectrum. The First does it with passion [Fire] while the other does it with logic [Air].

I have often seen this polarity on a much deeper level as well. I have seen it as, "unless one can know and understand themselves, they will never know, nor understand, The Other." To gain empathy, one must be in touch with oneself. Therefore, there is nothing quite as self-centered as the First House person, but this is because everything is filtered through him or her. Actually, First House people can be quite empathic, if they can personally relate to a given situation. This is the essence of the 1st/7th polarity: it's "how can I develop as an individual, so I can relate to you?"

This brings me directly into another side of Juno. Not all of the stories reveal her as the character played by Kathleen Turner in *The War of the Roses*. There is actually much to honor about Juno. If absolutely nothing else, she was a virtuous woman, who honored her marriage vows under adverse circumstances. It went further than that and was seen with great respect:

Homeric Hymn 12 to Hera
(translation by Evelyn-White) :
"I sing of golden-throned Hera whom Rhea bare. Queen of the Immortals is she, surpassing all in beauty: she is the sister and wife of loud-thundering Zeus—the glorious one whom all the blessed throughout high Olympos reverence and honour even as Zeus who delights in thunder."

As we continue to gain respect for our Seventh archtype, and quit treating her like an empty-headed, love-struck, giggling school-girl (i.e., a piece of fluff), we can bring her civilizing power and grace back into our culture and experience the full capacity of the Seventh. Juno is the goddess of marriage, and she was revered for her loyalty and fidelity. Her Greek name, Hera, is the feminine for hero. She was also titled as Lady. In earlier accounts, she was the Etruscan earth mother, or goddess of fertility, and in Rome, Juno was always regarded as the protectress of women. In *Fellini on Fellini* he shares some significant words.

> *"I believe that husbands should not oppress their wives, consider them private property, place them in slavery without real love...The wife must not be the Madonna, nor an instrument of pleasure, and least of all a servant."*

A strong Juno in a woman's chart will have her looking to a marriage and/or partnership to satisfy her main ambitions. Marriage, oftentimes, represents status and security.

The man with Juno strong in the relationship areas of his chart will most likely live in his marriage as a monogamous partner.

Now, with an expanded knowledge and understanding of this polarity of self and other, we have the promise of bringing about a more perfect union with another. We can honor our personal ego development—own our individuality—and subsequently respect The Other with equality.

Within this polarity, we can readily recreate this archetype into a new idea of conscious commitment, and perhaps even bring back an old/ancient idea and ideal that a personal marriage to another that can take us, without trepidation, into the intimacy of the Eighth archetype.

Early sculptures portray Hera as beautiful, poised, and vibrant. The beautiful peacock was sacred to her. It was said that Zeus/Jupiter wooed her in the form of a peacock. For in spite of all the bickering scenes in Homer's *Iliad*, in older cults they told of a transcendent encounter between these two on the top of Mount Ida, where, it was said that Zeus/Jupiter took his wife in his arms and the earth sent fresh grass beneath them. They laid themselves on a bed of hyacinths that lifted them off the ground and became one with the other. This "transcendence" is stepping from the Seventh into the Eighth.

Chapter **16**

The Eighth Archetype

Pluto/Mars-Scorpio-Eighth House
Water -Fixed- Succedent

Each of the Water signs—Cancer, Scorpio, and Pisces—is expressed with a distinct metaphor: Cancer is the formidable, lunar-controlled Ocean, Scorpio is The Swamp, shadowy and somber, and the enveloping, penetrating Fog belongs to Pisces. Each of these Water signs integrates the process that began with its respective Fire sign and establishes a fertile womb that will spawn the next process.

   With the Eighth, we've come to the end of the second—or Social—quartet of the Archetypes. As we did when we came to the end of the first [Personal] Quartet, let's try to get a feeling for what has transpired. If you recall, in Chapter 10 we examined this a bit and used the words; Courtship, Apprenticeship, Relationship, and Fusion. In this Eighth Archetype we've arrived at the Fusion phase of the Social Quartet... and all that it implies.

Let us look at some of the natural characteristics of water: it alters Fire by extinguishing fire; it can move dirt and wear away rock; and the components of air—two parts hydrogen and one part oxygen—are what make up water. By its essence, water is compliant, and it fills and conforms to its container; but it is the only one of the elements (Fire, Earth, Air, and Water) that can reflect back an accurate image of something outside of its self—similar to a mirror! The Water element is significantly complex.

Since The Eighth Archetype is the synthesis of becoming conscious (begun back at the Fifth Archetype), it is the area where all the conflicts laying dormant within the first synthesis — the subconscious mind—also come into consciousness. Each Water sign is not only the synthesis of the beginning Fire, but as well, each synthesizes the process that went before. If the process before is healthy, over all, then the subsequent process has the potential of being healthy. When I speak of health, I mean body, mind, and soul healthy… or, the lack of pathology in the body, the mental processes, and psychologically.

Just to keep personal guilt at bay, however, it can be expressed fairly accurately that there is none of us walking around in complete health. We have incorporated monsters in our lives, which have been passed down from generation to generation. In the Bible it is said that a person's sin will be carried onto nine future generations. Considering that the word sin in Greek means an error of judgment, originally used in their sport competitions, I suspect they had some inside psychological knowledge when that was expressed.

Nevertheless, these personal monsters, which seem to enjoy feeding on our psyches, are at the root of general health. Their subsistence comes to us in the form of words. These monstrous words, spoken to us on a subliminal level, can be brought into view with this Archetypal process. All of that which was developed in darkness (remember—everything from the First through the Sixth is under the Horizon—therefore, hidden) has moved into position by a commitment to an-other (the Seventh) to be mirrored back, facilitating a transformation of deeper, personal understanding, with the potential of raising one's consciousness.

In the Universe there is only one constant—One Law. That Law states that everything in the universe is in constant motion. This motion is the influx of change. Everything is transforming and transmuting, on some level, all the time. Within the Third Archetypal material, it was established that our material world is composed only of different combinations of energy called atoms. So, let's assume that all the combinations of atoms are in their unique position within a systematic process of moving toward one supreme, or dominant, combination of atoms—and that this total unification of all atoms into a central molecule combination is absolute Perfection, or the closest thing that can be conceived of as an omnipotent God. There seems to be a cosmic force that drives each molecule forward to this Central Unification of Perfection, which, in turn, keeps everything in constant motion.

There are parts of the Universe that are solid or dense. It's one theory that density—or what we consider as matter—is related to the notion of separateness. In other words, a rock can feel separated from the soil, and we can feel separated from each other and from the notion of God. As mentioned above, one of our innate drives is to connect, not only with another, but also with the Whole, or God. Therefore, under this hypothesis, what we call the real world is a dimension of the Universe that is heavily in the throes of struggle to eliminate the lonely feeling, or the concept of separateness.

Subsequently, since everything is going through this metamorphosis, there are infinite levels of connecting that are going on simultaneously just on this planet alone: rocks are breaking down, taking eons to transform and re-connect to another in the form of dirt; trees take hundreds of years to go through a single transformation—from seed to each year's growth. Humans, who are more aware of the non-physical, are working on a more ethereal level. We are conscious, and subsequently we are dealing with energy transformations on a non-physical level.

This process can be seen within different belief-systems —within reincarnation or one-life and one-death. If it's the first, then we can relate to the Easterner's concept of Karma; if we choose the latter, then we are on a plan to transcend the real world into a total transformation. A lot of people do seem to like the idea that we have more than one chance at this process into enlightenment; however, either one will give us the necessary delivery into the next phase that will start with the Ninth—the wellspring of religion.

Unless you have planets in Scorpio, Pluto prominent, i.e., on the Ascendant, or multiple planets placed in the Eighth House, you cannot grasp the profundity of what is forthcoming. One has to understand the depth of the Eighth Archetype's subliminal process. These Eighth Archetype-types have such intense feelings that oftentimes they may fear them; others, however, simply respect them. These people have learned to deal with this inner intensity early in life; however, each of us has some form of these intense feelings. In fact, we all need them, and most of all, we need to recognize the Eighth and the resulting intensity for what it is. This intensity is everything we fear within ourselves —the things that make us feel inferior. These feelings originated in the Fourth as seeds in our subconscious mind, which spawned our ability for consciousness in the Fifth, and then are brought to harvest in the adult's daily life through the interaction with a mate. The mate acts as a mirror, showing us what is prominent in our areas of separateness; only an intimate can get close enough to poke a ripping finger into our gaping wounds.

Another arena that provides a healing is a therapist's office. A counselor—whether trained therapist or psychologist or proficient astrologer—can offer a deeper understanding, through their schooling and knowledge; but therapy doesn't offer the same opportunity for healing that intimate love with a mate can. It is said that nothing can heal the earlier wounds better than a good, long-term, intimate marriage. Marriage in this context is different than the Seventh's conscious decision to be with another. This reference here is to intimacy.

This introduces the Second's Polarity of the Second and Eighth Archetype. The Second is my feelings, while the Eighth is our feelings. As well, the Second is how I feel, and the Eighth is how you make me feel. Therefore, mating—whether socially healthy or not—identifies our personal pain and gives us the opportunity to grow and transform. Even if the relationship is full of strife, and it is ultimately necessary, for the sake of our mental health, to dissolve the commitment, an objective reflection on our internal pain and fears can bring many of our personal issues to the surface. In other words, the very worst scenario can offer enough information about one's wounds to facilitate a process that can bring about a massive internal healing.

Moreover, it is through sexual intimacy that we can transcend the physical and actually become one with another! Those of us raised in the Judeo-Christian atmosphere have not really been provided with an adequate archetypal expression to completely embrace this concept openly. Most of our culture is focused more on the Second's concept of sexual interactions, my sexuality, which opposes the Eighth's our sexuality. The Eastern cultures have a huge provision in their religion for sexual intimacy. It is called Tantra.

Tantra is a Sanskrit word with a wealth of definitions and has emerged as the best single term for describing consciousness-raising sexual activity. For many Hindus and Buddhists it is a serious religious path; however, Tantra-type practices are known around the world. The Chinese, Native American, Polynesian, Egyptian, Scandinavian, and African cultures all have their own versions of Tantric sex. It transcends the physical body and becomes a union of the mind and soul.

Remember, however, that what is being clearly expressed here is intimacy and not promiscuity. If promiscuous sex comes out of this Archetype, then it is rooted in anger and it is pathological. To indicate that a Scorpio simply loves sex misses the mark on this individual, because it's Polarity, Taurus, is about values. Taurus is what I value, as Scorpio is what we come to value together.

Pluto meant riches to the Romans. Subsequently, the Second house is my money, while the Eighth house is our money. Of course, the latter can go into other territory such as inheritances, mortgages, loans, debts, and taxes. All of those areas include you, others and money... or what one values.

Let's focus on the fact that the Eighth is a synthesis of not only the Fifth, Sixth and Seventh Archetypes, but of the First through Fourth as well. The First, Second and Third encompass our primordial thrust into a physical reality, while the Fourth synthesizes that experience into a holding tank called the subconscious mind—the code that is set by our primal experiences.

The subconscious, according to *The MacMillan Dictionary,* is *"existing in the mind but not in consciousness... [the] portion of the mind that retains experiences and feelings that are difficult to bring back to awareness, often because awareness of them would be painful or produce anxiety."*

As we have learned, the subconscious forms the fountainhead of consciousness, and subsequently makes the Fifth Archetype dependent on the synthesis of the first four. The synthesis of the next process—the Fifth, Sixth, and Seventh into the Eighth—is, also, dependent on how well we developed the first.

According to Carl Jung in his Two Essays, *"The repressed content must be made conscious so as to produce a tension of opposites, without which no forward movement is possible."* He goes on to describe the conscious mind as being on top, while the *"shadow"* is underneath. He deems that *"high always longs for low and hot longs for cold, so all consciousness, perhaps without being aware of it, seeks its unconscious opposite ..."*

Consciousness is signified by light, and the subconscious —because it is out of the realm of accessibility—is dark, or shadowy. Within this synthesis, dark and light become one and the same...

Joseph Campbell talks about early mythology of Sumer. In these early records, Dumuzi-absu was the *"Faithful Son of the Abyss."* He was involved with two goddesses—or actually one goddess in two forms: one was the goddess of the living and the other was goddess of the dead. The goddess of the living was Inanna, Queen of Heaven, who, according to Campbell, *"became, in later Classical mythology, Aphrodite; and as the latter, she was the dreadful Queen of the Underworld, Ereshkigal, who became in Classical myth Persephone ..."*

The Eighth Archetype most blatantly brings about our inner polarity—that conflict that takes place with every human. The internal development brings about a dual personality, which lives within each of our minds and souls: the victim and the persecutor. Within each transformation, both of these characters must play their part. The drama must have both roles: the antagonist and the hero. Without the internal recognition of that battle, there can be no transformation.

As Pluto permeated our consciousness back in 1930 with the onset of WWII, the Jewish Holocaust, the atomic bomb, and psychoanalysis, it could only be a counterpart of the dark, ominous waters of Scorpio. The entire world was faced with its most feared shadow. The invading societies were raging with megalomania, while the conquered were faced with their most de-humanizing fears. Pluto came into our consciousness to bring us into the awareness that each of us has within us the dictator, the victim, and the hero. The very thing that makes the Eighth so ominous is nothing more than the complexities that began with what was manifested within its polarity—the Second—and which became a truth in the synthesis of the subconscious during our earliest days, months, and years of this life, whether planned from a previous life, or just being laid as the foundation for this one. Inanna is the earlier identity of Venus, which, of course, is the planetary ruler of the Second. When brought into her polarity to face Ereshkigal, she is stripped naked and brought to her knees. Ereshkigal has been brought into the consciousness of the modern human on the back of the planet Pluto.

A full account can be read in Liz Greene's *Astrology of Fate*. Brilliantly she says that this *"material is relevant enough to confirm my feeling that in the astrological Pluto we are confronting something feminine, primordial and matriarchal. When the goddess Inanna, the Sumerian Queen of Heaven...descends into her sister, Ereshkigal's realm... pieces of her clothing and regalia are ritually stripped at each of the underworld's seven gates."* Ms. Greene connects this scene with her personal and professional familiarity with Pluto progressions and transits *"— the gradual loss of everything which one has previously used to define one's identity and the 'bowing low' of humiliation, humility and eventual acceptance of something greater and more powerful than oneself."* It's been her experience that this phenomenon is present in both men and women.

I concur with Ms. Greene. This has been my professional and personal experience as well. When one is under the spell of the Eighth, as during a transit from Pluto, or because of placements in the natal chart, we often find ourselves feeling as though we are being ripped apart (I like a description I once heard: "as though our skin is being ripped off one inch at a time"). That state of mind is generally called neurosis.

Neurosis, in a most simple explanation, is not liking one's reality, which seems to cause an internal conflict with the individual and their environment. Carl Jung, in a series of talks given to a group of doctors in London in 1935, gives us a broader view of neurosis and its transformational and psychological functions, and makes a neurotic episode somewhat more palatable. He calls it *a "dissociation of personality due to the existence of complexes."* Nonetheless, he sees complexes as normal; however, there's the possibility that the complexes are incompatible with each other and *"that part of the personality which is too contrary to the conscious part becomes split off ..."* That "split-off" part dwells in the subconscious and cannot be dealt with directly. He goes on to make the logical claim that... *"Any incompatibility of character can cause dissociation, and too great a split between the thinking and the feeling function, for instance, is already a slight neurosis. When you are not quite at one with yourself in a given matter, you are approaching a neurotic condition."*

This awareness that a Pluto experience can generate, bringing one face to face with these internal demons, also known as the "split-off" part of oneself which lives and rules in the dark crevices of the subconscious—your personal Ereshkigal—can be the pathway to your own private transformation. Carl Jung concluded by saying, *"Neurosis is really an attempt at self-cure. It is an attempt for the self-regulating psychic system to restore the balance."*

Nevertheless, our personal episodes with neurosis are not always done in isolation. One can be solitary, choosing to be alone during the neurotic episode; but the genesis of a neurosis episode is not spawned in isolation. There has to be another to interact with, or most likely the neurosis lays dormant. The other normally acts as a mirror, triggering dormant wounds, either by their own behavior or by willfully pointing out our shadowed wounds by openly criticizing us. Both are equally disruptive.

Remember the Quadrant where we are working: Third Quadrant—Objective Awareness of Not-Self; Creative Release, Awareness of Others. In the Seventh we come above the Horizon and see the Other. In the Eighth, we take the reflection of ourselves into the integration of self-worth and accomplishment—or, we find the depth of our ineptitude and the self-hate within that reflection. Even if our mate is saying endearing things, within our own minds we can hear disputing words; but when anger flares and the words come out, those words that poke a probing finger into those wounds of fear and doubt, a loud inner-voice sounds confirmations in our heads, "See, I knew it!"

Liz Greene goes even deeper into this in *Astrology of Fate*. She tells us that whenever we're *"Confronted with Pluto, we meet our abhorrent compulsions, our unquenchable passions: the impossible repetitive pattern of struggling with something only to meet it again and again...He reminds us over and over of the incurable thing, the place of the unhealable wound, the psychopathic side of the personality..."*

Neither party is innocent, however; both are emanating from these lesions within their psyche...those sacred wounded places that are nurtured and protected, oftentimes sending one fleeing from one relationship into another to defend the wound from that ultimate journey into the light. This is where Mars arrives as the ancient ruler of Scorpio, for this becomes a fight to the death…Each person jockeys for control over the other; each feeling out of control, powerless and insignificant. Neither can acknowledge the "plank" in their own eye for seeing the "splinter" in the other's.

When we are faced with this part of ourselves – our pre-conceived inadequacies which transpired in the darkness of the chart's Northern Hemisphere—through the eyes, words and actions of that significant Other, emotionally we instinctively run in terror. This is the time-and-again time that we end up in the bar, or at our friend's kitchen table, with some sort of drink in front of us, saying to the person on the other side of the table, "You'll never guess what the bastard/bitch did to me this time!" We need someone (and oftentimes, ANYone) to stand between us and the Hydra, so that we don't have to look into its face… into the face that reflects our own inner hideousness. We will blame anyone, everyone, to keep from owning the monster as our own.

To me one of the best mythological examples of this Archetype is the story of Medusa. Medusa originally was a beautiful young woman whose crowning glory was her magnificent long hair. She was raped by Neptune (again a metaphor…perhaps illusion, delusion, fantasy, idealism). The end result transformed Medusa into a Gorgon, whose beautiful tresses turned into snakes and whose twisted outraged face turned men to stone.

Now the metaphor goes on. In both Greek and Roman mythology, Perseus, needing to rescue his mother Danae from King Polydectes, realized he needed Medusa's head to give him a powerful weapon to meet the challenge. With the help of Athena and Hermes—magic winged sandals, a cap, a pouch and a mirror-like shield, he fought her and beheaded her by viewing her image in the mirror of his shield rather than looking at her directly.

We could take each part of this into many avenues of depth —such as "rescuing the mother," "magic winged sandals," etc.— but the message I wish to focus on is the mirror-like shield. This introduces the absolute need for a mirror to enable us to behead our monsters. That mirror is inevitably that intimate relationship you have, on some unconscious level, attracted into your life that will give you the potential to kill the monster that holds the power of your bliss.

The awareness, however, is that we are looking into a mirror: we have to accept that this is a reflection of our self. When we acknowledge that this is our stuff, a spark of light that is beyond logic and rationale, emerges out of the repetition of our reflected image. In some sort of illuminating form, it must finally occur to us that what we are despising in the other is exactly what is blocking us on our pathway to Wholeness.

Before we can come to terms with taking responsibility for ourselves (which translates in any therapeutic environment as being "I create my life and decide how I want it to be"), we must go through years, or perhaps even lifetimes, of what is popularly termed co-dependency. It is said that co-dependent folks are controllers; but that's not difficult to grasp when we are dealing with the internal fears that we're actually seen as we really are. We attempt to control because recognizing that these internal fears are untrue would leave us stripped of what we perceive as our identity; but it ultimately offers the reward of growth and transformation.

This, subsequently, brings us to the attributes of Pluto entering into our consciousness within the 20th Century. With the breakthrough of the psychoanalytic process, and what its inception has propagated, this archetype has promising healing properties. Relative to Pluto's association with gifts and riches, I would like to bring in the words of James Hillman of *The Dream and the Underworld.* He gives the fullness to Pluto's ability when he says, *"Pluto, especially, is important to recognize in our euphemistic references to the unconscious as the giver of wholeness, a storehouse of abundant riches, a place not of fixation in torment, but a place, if propitiated rightly, that offers fertile plenty .."*.

What greater gift is there than a healing—a release—from the torture and torment of a neurosis! Moreover, what greater gift is there than total trust and intimacy with another. Isn't this what all of us secretly desire, with an internal yearning?

An illustrating and provocative poem by William Carlos

Williams follows…

The whole process is a lie,
unless,
crowned by excess,
It break forcefully,
one way or another,
from its confinement—
or find a deeper well.
Antony and Cleopatra
were right;
they have shown
the way. I love you
or I do not live
at all.

Daffodil time
is past. This is
summer, summer!
the heart says,
and not even the full of it.
No doubts
are permitted—
though they will come
and may
before our time
overwhelm us.
We are only mortal
but being mortal
can defy our fate.
We may
by an outside chance
even win! We do not
look to see
jonquils and violets
come again
but there are,
still, the roses!

Romance has no part in it.
The business of love is
cruelty which,
by our wills,
we transform
to live together.
It has its seasons,
for and against,
whatever the heart
fumbles in the dark
to assert
toward the end of May.
Just as the nature of briars
is to tear flesh,
I have proceeded
through them.
Keep
the briars out,
they say.
You cannot live
and keep free of
briars.

Children pick flowers.
Let them.
Though having them
in hand
they have no further use for them
but leave them crumpled
at the curb's edge.

At our age the imagination
across the sorry facts
lifts us
to make roses
stand before thorns.
Sure
love is cruel
and selfish

> *and totally obtuse—*
> *at least, blinded by the light,*
> *young love is.*
> *But we are older,*
> *I to love*
> *and you to be loved,*
> *we have,*
> *no matter how,*
> *by our wills survived*
> *to keep*
> *the jeweled prize*
> *always*
> *at our finger tips.*
> *We will it so*
> *and so it is*
>
> *past all accident.*

In conclusion, let us explore the polarity between Inanna and Ereshkigal…Venus and Persephone. It is this polarity that is the true generator of life. The Second Archetype is the primordial expression of the individual's experience of the physical senses. It is all of the things that our touch/smell/taste/sight/sound rejoice in. It is the wellspring of our security base, our innate system of what we value. As Liz Greene says in the *Astrology of Fate*, *"Inanna is an earlier and less differentiated form of Venus, goddess of sexual love and fertility. She is creative and joyful, the Queen of Heaven, unmarried and with many lovers, delighting in the beauty of her own body...seeking her fulfillment through stimulation from, and union with, beloved objects* [of pleasure]."

We can surely see the shallowness of the Second Archetype and its future without its polarity. Moreover, we can see it with any two-year-old who screams "Mine!" and who would easily shove the intruder—although possibly innocent—to his death, without a moment of remorse. We can also see the negative personification of this archetype within the stepmother in Walt Disney's *Snow White*...."Mirror, Mirror on the wall..." With only Venus, this would have little depth, and no meaningful connection to others.

As well, we have encountered Prosperpina's story back when we introduced her mother, Ceres, in the chapter on the Sixth Archetype. Prosperpina was the epitome of the above archetype, until she was kidnapped, taken to the Underworld and raped. Her senses were violated; her security was defiled; however, Prosperpina chose a time in the light and a time in the darkness... a time of heaven and a time of hell. Prosperpina went from the naiveté of a girl to the strength of womanhood. She left the shadow of her mother (Fourth Archetype and subconscious) and became a queen within her own right. Through her own pain, she gained the reward of transformation.

Chapter 17
The Ninth Archetype
Jupiter-Sagittarius-Ninth House
Fire- Mutable- Cadent

Actually, to be completely accurate about our Western philosophical/ religious origin, the story goes: In the beginning, there were the gatherers and the hunters. Initially, cult sites developed primarily for survival. The agrarians were the seed of civilization because it became necessary to develop a single site to reproduce food and store it for future survival. This developed into a worship of fertility which was more associated with the reproduction of the feminine; the cults were urbanized around fertile grounds – in our Western world it was around the Tigris/Euphrates and the Nile Rivers. Their early lives were ordered and worship was developed, and even sacrifices were prevalent, but war was not part of their life.

Nonetheless, even before the violent entry of the late Bronze and early Iron Age there were early nomadic cattle herders that came down from the north, as well as sheep and goat herders from the south that wandered into these ancient urbane areas. Joseph Campbell explains *"there had prevailed in that world an essentially organic, vegetal, non-heroic view of the nature and necessities of life that was completely repugnant to those lion hearts for whom not the patient toil of earth but the battle spear and its plunder were the source of both wealth and joy."* Initially in the older matriarchal myths and beliefs life was a thing of light and dark aspects which were respected equally and were joined together; whereas in the newer patriarchal myth "good" was attributed to new, heroic, master gods, thus leaving the natural primal elements to darkness – to which negative moral judgment was added. Subsequently, this put utmost conflict to the social order as the two factions of belief clashed. Where the goddess was worshiped as the giver and supporter of life, as well as the consumer of the dead, women, as her representatives had the prominent position in society. The Patriarchal opposition held a passion for righteous persuasiveness, with the fury of fire and sword. The conflict of the Patriarchy over the Matriarchy is aptly recorded in our known myths: the biblical account of Yahweh's victory over the serpent of the cosmic sea, Leviathan.

The counterpart for the Greeks was Zeus' victory over Typhon, the youngest child of Gaea, the goddess/Mother. He was an enormous half man, half snake, whose arms spread from sunrise to sunset and whose head, consisting of a hundred serpents, reached the stars. Voices could be heard from each serpent, along with hisses, sending out sounds only gods could understand; but too there were bellows like bulls, roars like lions and howls like dogs that were so loud that the mountains echoed.

These are a couple of references to the battles, and subsequent supremacy of the patriarchy over the matriarchy. Within this patriarchal rule, there has prevailed the quality of weakness concerning the Matriarchy and women in general.

The contrast of the two systems can be investigated within a more contemporary setting as when the Europeans settled the American continents, the above was reenacted. In spite of some aggressive "tribes," the Native American cultures could be regarded as more matriarchal in nature.

On the other hand, just as the Conscious development must conquer the Subconscious Mind in order to emerge, it is, metaphorically, the same procedure for the Eighth and Ninth Archetypes. Within the archetypal imagery of Zeus over Titan dominion, the battle fought with Typhon smacks remarkably of the life/death battle that one encounters when transmuting through the Eighth Archetype! While in the throes of an argumentative war with an intimate (a mate), who of us has not recognized those sounds that only the gods could understand: the bellowing like bulls, roaring like lions, baying like dogs, or even the hissing?

When we come face to face with the Hydra, and surface alive and victorious, that is when we emerge into The Truth, The Purpose of Our Plight. Simultaneously, when we know that the battle has ended, we have, as well, come to a clearer understanding. At that moment, we are standing at the threshold of the Ninth Archetype. We experience the transforming evidence that the spawning of the Ninth could only emerge from the murky waters of the Eighth.

The essence of this archetype is a driving force. Its fiery depths go to the belly of vital energy and its deep, rich hue is no less the color of Fire than with the Fiery dispositions of the First and Fifth Archetypes. Therefore, as with the first two Fire Archetypes, this position is one of ego development...or, the Ninth is also a development of the individualized personality—what is thought of as the self. Aries is "What Am I?," Leo is "Who Am I?" and Sagittarius is "Why Am I?"

As a result, the Ninth is the need to have a purpose in life, to have all of this stuff we call life mean something. It is to have the knowledge that our existence has meaning and directional purpose. The Ninth Archetype can be aptly titled: The search for the purpose of life.

There are two fundamental things to look at when undertaking a study of the Ninth Archetype. First is the fact that Sagittarius is a Mutable Sign and the Ninth is a Cadent House. This Archetypal development must be in a constant flux of change, for change is at the heart of its nature.

Secondly, the Ninth is still in the Third Quadrant of integration with The Other, while the process it creates embraces the entire Fourth Quadrant: Objective Awareness of Self. This last series of action contains the most complicated of all the rest. Just those words together generate an oxymoron: how can one be objective and aware of self? Of course, social integration, political power and spiritual identity gives us the proper clue, and we can readily see that this particular Quadrant thrusts us into situations where we must implement our internal development in the external world. This is the place—the series of action—that ultimately will expose the true nature of our character. It will reveal, for the entire world to see, exactly how we have progressed through the other three Quadrants.

It is interesting to look at exactly how the Quadrants and the Three Courses of Action interact. The Initial Course begins its characterization through the three houses of the First Quadrant, synthesizing within the first house of the Second Quadrant. The Intermediate Course of Action straddles equally the Second Quadrant and the Third Quadrant—the last two houses of the Second Quadrant and the beginning two houses of the Third Quadrant. That suggests that there's a dependency on counterbalance and adjustments.

The Finishing Course (the one we are entering here) begins with last house of the Third Quadrant; it still has its feet firmly planted in the reflective characteristic we encounter while looking into the face of The Other. If the Quadrants are a process as well, they are, then the Ninth is the culmination of joining with another with the motivation of obtaining self-understanding. This culminating process of the Third Quadrant, which starts with Cardinal Air, ends with an accumulation of life's in Mutable Fire. This ending also consummates a Fiery beginning into the Fourth Quadrant.

What we began with our interactions with others—as we gain an Objective Awareness of [the] Not-Self—we subsequently take onto and into our most elevated part of life and living. The Ninth sets us on our wondering quest; it is an innate drive to assimilate knowledge. Out of knowledge, we acquire a philosophy.

From a philosophic stance, we obtain a religion (or belief system). Religion becomes—and is—the wellspring of social customs. Laws are spawned from the social customs.

The Ninth is the domain of Long Black Robes: Priests, Judges, and Professors. And each of these positions in society tends to have one thing in common: each thinks/acts/believes that s/he has cornered the market on The Truth! This Truth can come in many forms. It comes when one seeks any type of knowledge and understanding. And since this Archetype's position is still solidly in the Third Quadrant, understanding is pursued outside of oneself. I have, therefore, christened The Ninth as "Ah-Ha! I see God and S/He looks just like me!" One can make this claim because, even though we suppose that we are looking outside of ourselves, the Third Quadrant's outside source can only concisely reflect our inner development.

The Ninth can be best scrutinized within the framework of religion. If one looks at religion with some objectivity—not through the restricting eyes of their introspective, dogmatic beliefs —we can see that they all have one thing in common. Whether it is within different sects of the same religion, or whether we observe the unambiguous differences of world religions, such as Hinduism, Buddhism, Christianity, Islam—or some obscure belief system of a hidden tribe in a rainforest—each of them holds its own as The Truth. Moreover, each has documentation, and above all, testimony, which proves, without a doubt, that their belief is the true belief.

I want to point out, however, that this area of life has little to do with the development of spirituality. For the sake of clarity, I shall paraphrase an explanation of the difference between spirituality and religiosity that I heard from Rob Hand. Religion is a structure; it tells where God lives, how to find where God lives, what God looks like, His/Her dimensions, what Heaven is, where Heaven is, and all the acts, thoughts and deeds to get to see God and/or live in Heaven, or its equivalent. Spirituality, on the other hand, is harmoniously aligning your energy with natural or cosmic energy—which is accomplished through a fervid awareness of oneself outside of them; one who is functioning serenely within the world, but not in the world. This is the essential concern of the Twelfth Archetype.

Simply being affluent in the Ninth doesn't automatically create an alliance with the Twelfth. As a matter of fact, this area of religion is in a square (90° aspect) to spirituality. This clearly indicates, as with any square aspect, that certain adjustments must be made to obtain harmony in both areas. Since Fire is definitely an ego development, and Water is the assimilation of the ego into a greater whole, the square's conflict is evident!

On the other hand, each supporter of any of the above religions has a personal faith based on their particular concept of its teachings. Even though the dogma of a religion may be the foundation of one's Belief System, its integration into one's life is extremely personal. The Ninth is, subsequently, the core of an individual's faith. Faith is a necessary element of functioning. Without faith, one can't get out of bed in the morning. Without faith it's impossible to function. That can be seen when one looks into the eyes of the extremely depressed.

Since everything within all the Twelve Archetypes is part of a complete process of human development, one can certainly find solace in the Ninth, and eventually get into alignment so that one may enter the higher purpose of the Twelfth. One can take the faith, which is formed through a personal connection with a religion, and use it to connect to something deeper. Many people find solace in their religious beliefs; but it must be brought into personal significance. As long as it remains in the hands of the Other, and it is not taken into the next, Subjective Quadrant, then it cannot take you into the higher realms of the Twelfth.

Within this context, the concept of Faith is interchangeable with the concept of being optimistic. Without the Faith—the internal belief—that I can accomplish, I cannot, will not, go forward. I will stay stuck in the inertia of fear or guilt…or both. The first two ego stages of development are beneath the Horizon—totally subjective. This stage energizes the confidence, which is needed for the delicate ego to be vigorously thrust out into the world.

Over-confidence, however, can generate arrogance. This arrogant potential is reflected in the physical composition of the Ninth's planet. Huge and majestic Jupiter—the largest planet in our solar system—is three hundred times more massive than the earth, but he is little more than a hot-air balloon. Composed mostly of hydrogen and helium, Jupiter possibly has little solid surface. Its gaseous material simply gets denser with depth, and what we see when we look at the planet, are the tops of clouds, high in the atmosphere.

This aptly reflects the delusion of grandeur that goes with the Ninth. And delusion is an appropriate word here. Jupiter's size is deceptive in the same way that our beautiful, blue sky deceives us into thinking that it is the outer limit of the universe. Subsequently, the sky is an appropriate metaphor for the Ninth. When one thinks of the sky, one can see clearly, that even though we think that it is the end of existence, it really isn't. There is no dome that fits snugly over the top of us, making us eternally safe and secure from any other possible reality, apart from that of our world.

Another way of seeing the sky metaphor is looking at the occasion when one gets too far above the rest. Sometimes, the better one is educated, or the more knowledge one has, the more they tend to be set apart from the rest of the group. In some cases, it gives them the delusion that they are set apart. When one actually sees, or believes that they can see a higher dimension or greater spectrum, they don't always adhere to the same moral code as those who do not experience equally from their level.

As a result, the person with a strong Ninth in their horoscope can often appear amoral to others. And often, many who follow their Ninth Archetype into the rationale of their Truth, are amoral! Joseph Campbell succinctly brings this home: *"We have already watched Olympian Zeus conquer the serpent son and consort of the goddess-mother Gaea. Let us now observe his behavior toward the numerous pretty young goddesses he met when he came, as it were, to gay Paree. Everyone has read of his mad turning of himself into bulls, serpents, swans, and showers*

of gold. Every Mediterranean nymph he saw set him crazy..."
More than one Sagittarian has followed his Father Zeus into
amoral behavior and promiscuity. Most of us can bring to mind
the example of so many religious leaders!

On the other hand, the Ninth has a succinct purpose. We
have to acquire a belief system; moreover, we have to believe in
our lives, our purpose and ourselves. If we don't believe we can
do something, then sure enough we can't. And just like Jupiter's
surface, this belief—our optimism—is fragile. With optimism, we
can succeed; without optimism, we will surely fail. The Greek
name for Jupiter is Zeus, which means Lightener, or one who
gives enlightenment. He is the Great Sky Father, the giver of gifts.
If one gets into a plane to go up as high as they can, the view is
normally tremendous. As the popular song goes, "I can see for
miles and miles and miles and miles..."

Jupiter is BIG! It's e x p a n s i v e! Since our reality
is based on our perception, which is made up of thoughts and,
subsequently, words–which is our Third Archetype–it stands
to reason that when all those thoughts and words flow into its
polarity it would be expansive.

The central focus here is that they both communicate.
Gemini says, "I acquire pieces of data," and Sagittarius takes
those pieces of data to create a concept. The Third deals with the
ABCs, which equates to elementary education, while the Ninth
takes the concepts and turns them into a philosophy (or Truth),
which is taught as a higher education. As well, the Third House
takes us around our environment gathering data, which is called
short journeys. The Ninth House travels far and wide, looking for
the ultimate Truth, and that is called long journeys.

Soaring with Zeus can indeed give one a dimension
through travel, education and delving into deeper understanding
that is unequaled in any other area of life. This, indeed, is a state
of becoming enlightened.

Chapter *18*

The Tenth Archetype
Saturn~Capricorn~Tenth House
Earth~ Cardinal~ Angular

What Fire has created, Earth brings into solid materialism.

Going back again and utilizing the images within the synthesis that took place in the Eighth, one can safely affirm that at that point we came face to face with our own mortality. Many scientific, theologic, and philosophic scholars have determined that it is this particular bit of information that sets us apart from the other species that inhabit our planet, and subsequently makes us conscious. Since the Eighth's synthesis brings us the awareness of our mortality, without the development of the Ninth, there would be no life—we would all jump from the nearest high place and be done with it. Becoming aware of the life/death process, without purpose, is depressing. Obviously, this brings us to a time when we would look outside of ourselves for answers. Interestingly enough, we have only one Fire and one Earth above the Horizon (while there are two Airs and two Waters above the Horizon). Therefore, if the Ninth Archetype has creatively emerged into the light giving us The Truth, then, as Liz Greene said, that this powerful Earth position is the *"law-giving principle which limits and structures worldly life."*

Out of the customs and laws of every religious belief, a social structure arises. We can boil it down to this statement: a person's creed structures their life. This is true for the macro-entity, as well as for the micro-entity. The central component in every coterie, and the governance that binds it, is a belief system that equates to a religion. A social order is spawned out of a collective concept of The Truth. And that development is the controlling factor of a particular society. It regulates the politics, the economy, and the morals of each and every congregation of peoples.

Saturn, or Kronos to the Greeks, was an earth god. He and Rhea, his consort, were born of the earth-mother, Gaia, from a union between the earth-mother and the sky-father Ouranos. Along with Kronos were born Oceanus, Coeus, Creus, Hyperion, Iapetur (brothers and sisters), Theis, Themis, Mnemosyne, Phoebe, and Tethyia–Twelve Titans in all. They were hideous, horrible things and were hated by their father. He banished them all to Tartaros, which is a place very much like the Christian hell.

Kronos took rulership from his father, Ouranos, by castrating him (this story was shared in more detail in the chapter on the Second Archetype). Then he became so ambitiously controlling that he didn't trust his own offspring; Saturn became so fearful and paranoid that he devoured his children—he swallowed them up! From this secure position, he ruled the Titans, without the knowledge that Rhea had hidden Zeus away. His rule in Tartaros was one of fear and dread. Within the Greek belief structure, the Titans were the personification of earthquakes and volcanic eruptions, and actually, their rudimentary position was as representatives of the wild forces of nature.

Later, Zeus attacked his father with the same zeal that Kronos had attacked Ouranos. After he freed his siblings from Kronos' stomach, the Olympian gods/goddesses reigned with a more genteel hand.

This story offers so many metaphors that it boggles the mind to know where to begin! The fear that history will repeat itself is a common fear of the Tenth Archetype. Significant concentration is applied in making sure a wrong is never repeated, to the point of devouring their offspring—whether it is their inner child's creativity, or their physical child.

Another metaphor is that an error in judgment can bring great sorrow. It also seems very metaphoric that the son who conquered him in all his fury was Zeus, or Jupiter—the archetypal image of the Ninth. There is much room for pondering here, an exploration that takes us into interesting vestibules. Just the combination of the two archetypal energies is intriguing; let's look at optimism on one hand, and pessimism on the other. The combination of these two energies can result in periods of euphoria and exhilaration, sandwiched between intervals of depression.

As well, a statement is being made about the Fourth/Tenth polarity. Our need for structure is preceded only by being born and having a mother. The Fourth Archetype is the representation of Gaia, and Gaia is the mother of Kronos. Then subsequently, all other archetypal deities within the astrological paradigm were Kronos' offspring, or subsequent offspring, except for Venus/Aphrodite, who is actually Kronos' sister by virtue of the fact that she was conceived from Ouranos' severed genitals when Kronos flung them into the sea. Moreover, so were the Erinyes or Furies. These little creatures are above the laws of the gods, and it's their essential purpose to hound the guilt-ridden mind into madness. This is certainly a Capricornian byproduct.

Many astrologers acquire clients when someone is having a Saturn transit. Saturn tests the structure —the very backbone — of one's life. I see Saturn as a big, fat man, somewhat pear-shaped, wearing an old black suit, rumpled, white shirt, narrow black tie, and scuffed black shoes. In his left hand is a worn, leather briefcase—the kind that is closed by a flap over the top, and with a buckle that fastens it shut on the front side. In his right hand is a tire iron. He rings your doorbell, and even though you answer with the warmest regard, he shows you no friendliness. You invite him in; you have been preparing for him for the past seven years, so you're feeling more confident than when he came to inspect before. He briskly passes you and walks to a beautiful wall, with pictures and a nice table with a vase of flowers. With one harsh blow of his tire iron, he lays a gaping hole in the wall. Pictures fall to the floor, and the breaking glass is joined by splashing water and scattered flowers. The hole reveals what is behind the exterior wall and its decoration. "Bad wiring…" he says, in a near monotone.

Starting with the Northern Hemisphere and moving above the horizon into the Southern Hemisphere, the order of the polarities, thus far, are Fire/Air, Earth/Water, Air/Fire, and now we come to Water/Earth. So, using our original paradigm about these elements, with the First Polarity, the Fire created (the Self) and the Air conceptualized (the Self as seen through the Other). Then, with the Second Polarity, the Earth manifested the personal attachment to the physical world, while the Water synthesized this attachment and transformed it so it can be released. With the Third Polarity, the Air conceptualized the physical world, and the Fire created a purpose —a meaning —for its existence.

The Fourth Polarity can be analyzed in a similar fashion. The Fourth Archetype synthesizes the personal experience of life, while the Tenth manifests the function of one's life experiences. The Fourth House is the interaction with one's family, including one's upbringing. The Tenth House is one's interaction in the world, including one's career. The Fourth is one's development to become; the Tenth is what one is becoming. This is why Saturn's cycles tend to mark milestones in people's lives.

As my mentor, Zipporah Dobyns, would say, "Saturn always calls for a reality check." He comes into your life, either through your natal chart, or by a transit, to bring you into reality. It's oftentimes difficult to know if one is suffering from Saturn or Pluto; both planets seem to destroy. The difference, though, is that Pluto's message is more nebulous as he brings us down to our knees. There is nothing nebulous about Saturn's message, as he is bringing us to our knees—most times it's obvious what we need to do. We have to get a better job, or get out of a bad relationship, or pay our bills on time, and obey the traffic laws. Saturn wants us to get the most out of our incarnation into this physical form; his dominion is circumscription.

Saturn is mostly known as a malefic planet, especially in traditional astrology. While Jupiter is jolly and fun, Saturn is serious and somber and grim. Liz Green tells us in *Saturn: A New Look at an Old Devil*, *"He is usually considered to be the bringer of limitation, frustration, hard work, and self-denial, and even his bright side is usually associated with wisdom and the self-discipline of the man who keeps his nose to the grindstone..."* Wherever Saturn or Capricorn is located is where you can surmise that you will need to apply focus, as well as have set-backs. I have Capricorn on my 9th house cusp, and distant travel has always been difficult, or absolutely withheld. On the other hand I have Jupiter in Sagittarius; therefore a personal conundrum. According to Ms. Greene's above text, Saturn is often referred to as the *"Lord of Karma."* However, she goes on to tell us that *"most ancient and persistent of teachings...tells us that he is the Dweller at the Threshold, the keeper of the keys to the gate, and that it is through him alone that we may achieve eventual freedom through self-understanding."*

Saturn is the barometer of maturity. It is through the maturation process that we obtain true freedom and self-understanding. It is said that a person hasn't truly grown-up until he has had his Saturn Return. That is when Saturn has returned to the exact position it was in when one was born. The first time that happens is about age 29.

Saturn has made some hallmark visits along the way. The first, or waxing Square, at age six or seven is when we realize that we are going to be required to person-ally relate to a social order, and to actually go to school and learn; the opposition happens at 14 or 15 when it seems that our parents, or other authority figures are constantly "on our case," and it seems that every time we turn around, we're in trouble again. Then, we must face the waning, or last square, at 21 when we're oftentimes tossed out into the cold, cruel world. With the latter, we are also having our first Uranus/Uranus square, and it is often the time when we think we're grown. At this point, we either spend the distance from that last, waning square to the final return rebelling against Daddy (or the archetypal Daddy of society), or conforming to what Daddy expects of us. As we do grow up, Saturn, with his tire iron, sees that we take all of these things into consideration.

Oftentimes, Saturn does show us where there may be issues with the father. A theme that is paramount in stories of Saturn is the battle between the father and the son. There are several stories around the necessity of killing the father-king—this is the ancient motif of the sacrificed king to secure the fertility of the crops. Again, Liz Greene tells us, *"The ancient symbol of king-sacrifice is also newer than we might think, for it is present in the figure of Christ, the Son of God and the King of the Jews. He was born (like all sacrificial king-redeemers) at the winter solstice, a birthday he shares with Mithra, Tammuz, Adonis and even King Arthur."*

Winter is the most obvious time of transition in our northern hemisphere. It is a time when life goes dormant, becomes introspective, and dies—or gives the impression of death. However, there is not a true death taking place, but rather, there is much transpiring. The activity that is happening is the preparation for the ultimate harvest, which will take place the next autumn. This process is done in darkness, either the darkness from the waning Sun, or the darkness of decomposition. This can easily be metaphoric of the executive of the company or country, sitting long and often dark hours in the office, breaking down old ideas, pondering the possibilities of new life, and weighing what is productive and what must be completely discarded. To the observing eye, it appears nothing is happening; but the future of life itself is coming about.

To stay in a perpetual winter would be a certain death, however—not only for us, but as well, for our planet as we know it. As well, to stay in a static social system also means certain death. The Tenth must be seen as a place of continual progress. People experiencing a Saturn transit, or those with strong natal Saturn or excessive Capricorn oftentimes see life as a half empty glass. The pain of depression can be a frequent companion; however, it's psychologically noted that depression is usually suppressed anger. This is where the knowledge that Mars is exalted in Capricorn can be essential. It's not significant here where Mars is in the chart; the significance here is that one suffering from this difficulty know that Martian energy can save the day, either through anger, or activity, or both. I'm not suggesting that one start a war, nor retaliate. I'm simply pointing out that this energy can bring about substantial personal change that can lead to accomplishment.

Let's remember that this Earth position represents the highest state of productivity. It is a Cardinal Sign, and an Angular House —a place of beginnings, of transition. This reveals a more positive view of the Tenth Archetype. Its potential signifies the presence of accomplishment and the fulfillment of recognition. This is the up side of Saturn. We have a need to succeed, a need to manifest positive results that are recognized by our community— the clan. We are driven for recognition in our field and that drive can lead to wholeness.

The activity of work and career are completely different. A man might be a mechanic from Monday morning until Friday at 5 P.M., at which time, he showers, puts on special clothes, and goes to play in a Rock 'n' Roll band. The former is his work, the latter his career. He does one for survival, and the other for wholeness, which brings him into completeness. If one's work isn't making him whole, then it is not a career.

Therefore we can think of the Midheaven, our career, as what we are becoming —the ultimate fulfillment of our self. Liz Greene says that *A New Look At An Old Devil,* that *"The state of wholeness is symbolized by what is called the archetype of the Self. This symbol does not suggest perfection...but instead implies completeness, where every human quality has its place and is contained in a harmonious way within the whole."* This archetype symbolizes the process of self-comprehension. Liz goes on to say, *"Saturn is connected with the educational value of pain and with the difference between external values —those that we acquire from others—and internal values—those that we have worked to discover within ourselves."*

Many of us often wear the garb of guilt and self-loathing that was the curse superimposed upon us by some actual or nebulous Other, which turned the vision of ourselves from acceptance into rejection. We have gone through that pain of lack and doubt, meeting that ogre again and again, in the darkness of doubt and depression. We can either become its servant, to be devoured in the darkness. Or, like Beowulf in his First Battle when he conquers Grendel—"an outcast of society"—we can tear its arm from its shoulder (the part of its body that holds and controls) and allow the life to drain from its body... claiming our victory. Liz Greene talks about how this archetype presents itself as the Beast in many fairy tales: *"Saturn's role as the Beast is a necessary aspect of his meaning, for as the fairy tale tells us, it is only when the Beast is loved for his own sake that he can be freed from the spell and can become the Prince."*

Until we can claim our position in society as our own, displaying our progress of accomplishments with pride, we will walk among the world as the Beast. The Ninth's potential dogma can invite us to take on a burden of guilt when we reach the Tenth. This happens when we allow the Ninth to be governed by the Other, instead of realizing that the entire process of the Third Quadrant is to be integrated into personal development as one enters the Fourth Quadrant.

Nevertheless, this guilt can be so heavy that unless we release it—leave it behind—we can never be free enough to be the Prince or Princess. The heavy, oppressive side of the Tenth help's us grow to this full potential of personal development. If a thing hurts enough, we will stop doing it; but as well, if we can gain recognition from the world for our efforts, we will strive to do that, too. Both of these are the Tenth's promise.

It is the energy that changes the world. Saturn and his mythological son, Jupiter are the venue for the world scene. In her *Book of Saturn*, Zip Dobyns said, *"...Jupiter and Saturn are conjunct, in the same degree in the sky, approximately every twenty years. The general patterns in the sky at these conjunctions were interpreted as clues to the nature of the next twenty years for the society. Early astrologers were interested in the general situation in their immediate world ... "* Jupiter/Saturn conjunctions are quite significant in Mundane Astrology. Charts calculated for those times are considered momentous for world events.

It is said that those born with a Jupiter/Saturn conjunction will be the leaders of new ideas. To give two brief examples, we can look at the lives of John Lennon and Bob Dylan. It was pointed out earlier that the Ninth and Tenth Archetypes are the only representatives of Fire and Earth above the Horizon. In the creation of this Fire and the manifestation of this Earth, we can bring about a better world —personally, as well as socially.

Chapter 19

The Eleventh Archetype

Uranus - Aquarius - Eleventh House
Air - Fixed - Succedent

Long before I could identify the face that went with the name Richard Tarnas, Barbara Morgan of I.S.I.S. handed me a copy of an essay he had written and told me to read it. That was either in 1987 or 1988. The essay was "The Archetypal Meaning of the Planet Uranus."

Barbara gave me the essay because, at that time, I'd already been teaching astrology for a couple of years at Southern Oregon State College (SOSC) in Ashland, Oregon, and I was heavily involved with creating similar material. Before I left Houston, I worked at a large astrological bookstore. It wasn't long before I found the works of people such as Stephen Arroyo and Liz Greene. It was Liz Greene, a Jungian astrologer, who initially introduced me to Jungian psychology. For me, it was like finding the Rosetta Stone. All the training I'd had in the Freudian model, plus all that I'd been developing over the years, suddenly found form... Ram Dass had become a major figure in my approach to life during the early '70s, and remember that studying with Zip Dobyns gave me the 12-Letter Alphabet. Although I couldn't be sure where I was going with it at the time, right before I left for Ashland, The book *The Astrology of Fate* rolled off the presses. When I began teaching at SOSC, I wanted my students to have a depth of understanding, not just disjointed parts. Yet, it had to come through an amalgamation all of my experiences. As I started teaching, by necessity my work on this archetypal material started to evolve.

When I came around the top of the chart, I suddenly was stopped dead in my tracks. All of the stories generated out of mythology fit their astrological counterpart, except for Uranus. Uranus, or Ouranos, was the sky god, and there wasn't much to be found about him or his characteristics. Actually, the most I could find about him was that he sired the Titans with the earth, Gaia, who was his sister, wife, and mother. He despised his offspring and banished them all to Tartaros, which was in the *"bowels of the underworld, so that they would not offend his aesthetic eye..."*

Uranus played another important part in Western mythology, when Kronos/Saturn severed his genitals and tossed them into the ocean, bringing forth Aphrodite/Venus from the foaming sea, and the Erinyes from the drops of blood. The Erinyes or Errinyes were also called the *"dogs of Hades."* They were the goddesses of vengeance, punishing those who had broken oaths, or murdered family members. In Hesiod's cosmogony they came forth from the drops of blood of the castrated Ouranos/Uranus. Their punishment was to drive their victims mad. But that was the extent of what I could find about this god, and try as I might, I couldn't make that fit into what I knew to be certain about the Eleventh Archetype. This is when Dr. Tarnas' paper became the clarification. Bear with me while I share his work with you. Without his work, the Eleventh Archetype cannot be brought into a modern archetypal interpretation. In his subsequent book (that was birthed from this original paper) *Prometheus, The Awakener*—a book I recommend to fully understand this chapter—he explains his reasoning, saying that the original seven planets were believed by the ancients to be an absolute cosmic structure, *"reflecting the primordial forces that governed human affairs."* However, this was not the case when Uranus was named by William Herschel, who was a musician and an amateur astronomer. Richard says that he suspects that 'Ouranos' was the logical name because he was the father of the preceding planet, Saturn, just as Saturn was the father of Jupiter. Too, according to Hesiod, "Ouranos" was the god of*"the starry sky."*

Still relating to Tarnas' book, he addresses the fact that when 20th Century astrologer explored the character of Uranus as a force "that governed human affairs," they found that it was very different from the mythological "Ouranos." As he put it, there is a *"...clear consensus among contemporary astrologers that the planet Uranus is empirically associated with the principle of change, rebellion, freedom, liberation, reform and revolution, and the unexpected breakup of structures; with excitement, sudden surprises, lightning-like flashes of insight, revelations and awakenings; and with intellectual brilliance, invention, creativity, originality and individualism."* As all astrologers know—as well as anyone who has been made aware—Uranus transits can reflect unpredictable and disruptive changes in one's life, along with sudden breakthroughs and liberating events. Subsequently, there is nothing in the mythology of "Ouranos" which would intimate radical change, rebellion, or intelligent brilliance; however, Richard skillfully noticed that these qualities definitely, and precisely, fit another within the Greek pantheon: Prometheus. Prometheus was the titan who rebelled against his fellow deities…

Taking a closer look at the story of Prometheus, he was the son of Iapetus (a Titan) and Clymene. It was believed that he created the first mortals from clay and water, after which the goddess Athene breathed life into them. Prometheus was originally portrayed as a primitive trickster-figure bent on out-witting the gods. Later, however, Aeschylus developed him into a culture hero, a figure who endures suffering for a noble cause, the champion of humanity. He took it upon himself to teach them skills and to help them develop. Zeus was not overly fond of the human race and really wanted them eliminated. It was his notion to create something better, perhaps envious of Prometheus' role in their creation. He only spared them because Prometheus pleaded their cause. This lament from the chorus in Aeschylus' **Prometheus Bound** expresses his dilemma:

> *You defiant, Prometheus, and your spirit*
> *In spite of all your pain, yields not an inch.*
> *But there is too much freedom in your words.*

> *Prometheus later responds:*

> *Oh, it is easy for the one who stands outside*
> *The prison wall of pain to exhort and*
> *teach the one who suffers.*

A primary story about Prometheus was when he asked to mediate in a dispute about which parts of a sacrificed bull should be served to the gods, and which part should be given to the humans to eat. He skinned the bull and made two bags from its hide. In one he put the best meat, concealed beneath the stomach, giving that one to the humans. In the bag for the gods, he put the bones and undesirable organs, but well hidden underneath a juicy layer of fat. Prometheus laughed with gusto when Zeus fell for the trick which made Zeus very angry. He punished Prometheus by withholding fire from humanity. In defiance, Prometheus went secretly to Olympus, stole back the precious glowing coal, hid it in a fennel-stalk and stole away, returning the fire to mankind.

When he discovered what Prometheus had done, Zeus retaliated by making a beautiful woman from clay named Pandora, complete with her famous box full of woes for mankind. He sent her to Prometheus' brother Epimetheus, who refused her, as Prometheus had already warned him against accepting gifts from Zeus. Foiled yet again, Zeus became even angrier; he made a final gesture of his supremacy by chaining Prometheus to a rock, and setting the tormenting griffon upon him. Prometheus stayed there unrelenting, until Chiron changed places with him.

In mythology there is no question of Prometheus' superior intellect; however, his intelligence is directly associated with humans and their development. As it is told in the stories, his intimate association to humanity gave him a deeper identity with their basic plight than the average inhabitant of the Greek Pantheon. This seems to mark him and humans as being on one side of a Cold War, while the gods and goddesses were on the other.

There are a number of significant archetypal inferences in the above story. First of all, the theme that Prometheus is most remembered for is the bringer of fire. Looking back with a historian's eye and considering the start of civilizing the human species, our earliest social developments are associated with securing a source of fire. Fire allowed our more primitive ancestors to have a better life than their other roaming primate contemporaries. They could cook their kill and keep it edible longer. They could warm themselves when suffering from the elements; likewise, fire would light their way into otherwise dark and forbidding places, such as caves, gaining added protection from the elements and predators. This would have been an impetus of social groups, since a lone fire could meet the needs of many individuals.

The Eleventh Archetype finds itself in Fixed Yang Polarity with the Fifth Archetype. Fixed Second Quadrant Fire finds both its antagonism and its fulfillment in Fixed Forth Quadrant Air. In considering this important dynamic, thoughts of the egoic identity completing itself by valuable social action makes clear a significant characteristic of this polarity. Prometheus stole fire, and the fire he stole was the fire of the sun. It was his objective to improve the life of humankind. The analogy is clear. The Eleventh Archetype is about, in part, taking the burning self and committing it to warm humanity at large.

Bringing into play the archetypal characteristics of Prometheus gives us an even deeper understanding of this picture. Prometheus' position in mythology is one of sacrifice, but unlike

Pisces, he does not sacrifice in the role of the victim. He is constantly the troublemaker—the Awakener. The very name Prometheus means foresight. And with those qualities in mind, Prometheus easily opens us up to the understanding of the eccentricity of the Uranian individual, along with the ideals that link one Aquarian to another, and as well, the bonding capabilities of the Eleventh House.

Strong Uranians have been considered eccentric and individualistic, while Aquarius is conscious of the social group, or clique. The Eleventh House is groups and organizations, as well as one's hopes and wishes. The deeper inspection, however, reveals that an individual process does not drive the Uranian, but rather, he is driven by a force that seems to be outside him —or, as Liz Geene says in *The Art of Stealing Fire,* *"... a force within the psyche that has access to knowledge of how the cosmic system works, and how to apply it to the everyday affairs of human beings."*

It takes a deep concentration to actually see the metaphor of the triplets (used earlier in this book) in this Archetype; one may not actually see the triplets as identical. Nonetheless, the identity is consistent. That is also true with the group, whether it be a group of rebels inciting a riot, or a garden club focusing on the beautification of the community; it is still a movement larger than the single individual. The Eleventh is in the middle of the Fourth Quadrant, and therefore, is the individual playing their role out in the world. And one's hopes and wishes can also be interpreted in this context, as was demonstrated when Uranus was discovered.

To demonstrate let's look closer to the development of our constitution. The delegates who came together in 1778 were from all walks of life—from urban gentlemen to settlers besieged by the wilds. Nonetheless, together these individuals from the edge of a wilderness were to bring about one of the most extraordinary political applications in the history of Western civilization.

Hopes and wishes are generated by the drive and ultimate fulfillment of a cause. If one does not possess that zeal—an internal drive—then what one hopes and wishes for will not come into being. That drive, however, doesn't come from an individual concept, but rather from a movement that seems to be bigger than the individual. It is like a fire in one's belly, that will take one into unknown territory, and into personal danger...sometimes resulting in death itself.

Liz Greene talks about hearing astrologers describe Uranus as "the planet of individuality," which would indicate someone different than you and me—someone with an "internal blueprint" that would be different than anyone else's. She clarifies that misinterpretation by saying, *Uranus is an outer planet. Because the outer planets reflect movements within the collective psyche, in which we all share, Uranus is not concerned with individual development. It may even prove inimical to individual values and individual emotional needs... because the individual is submerged in the group.*

Remembering that each polarity is not different energy, but rather the same energy in opposition, with Liz Greene's words we can get a clearer understanding of the Fifth/ Eleventh polarity: in the Fifth, one is becoming conscious of one's self; in the Eleventh, one is becoming conscious of one's place in the world.

Fire has been considered sacred well into more modern times; Greek temples were built and priestesses were kept so they could maintain the regional fire. Carefully, the embers were carried from the old province to the new settlement. Fire and its successors—from electricity to rocket fuel—continue to be worshiped. It allows us to store food and use our minds for creative purposes, rather than for base survival; it allows us to incorporate the entire planet into our immediate circle of fire, either by travel, or electronic communication; it defies darkness and can bring us continuous light. It is the constant that makes our world exist; it allows us to contemplate, and consequently to become conscious.

In the astrological paradigm, the First Archetype is becoming conscious of the body and the physical world; the Fifth is becoming conscious of the self and our individuality; and the Ninth is becoming conscious of our purpose and its meaning. And Air conceptualizes what Fire creates.

Liz Green refers to the importance of Rick Tarnas'

theme of Prometheus' fire in her book with *"the creative spark, cultural and technological breakthrough, the enhancement of human autonomy, the liberating gift from the heavens, sudden enlightenment, intellectual and spiritual awakening"*; but she deepens the metaphor to the concept of stealing *"the potential of consciousness from the gods."* Fire is solar and within that archetype (the Fifth) is the awareness of the Self. The Fifth is also imagination, creativity and the vision of making oneself known.

To further substantiate the symbology of Prometheus' fire, Melanie Reinhart, in *Chiron and the Healing Journey* also speaks about how it represents bringing *"enlightenment of consciousness to the human race."* But the depth of her insight carries on into the complexities of Prometheus' nature that so accurately relates to the nature of the planet Uranus' influence in one's horoscope. She talks about *"healthy rebellion against inhuman or superpersonal authority..."* Not only did Prometheus disregard authority, he showed little respect for the gods and even attempted to *"cheat and humiliate them."*

This, however, is not without consequence. To be elevated to this level of consciousness defies the gods and puts humanity into the role of a creative associate, rather than the servant. God is no longer worshipped submissively, and neither is the status quo. That behavior reflected in the Promethean/Uranian chart time and again brings the personality physical or mental punishment at its end. Strong emphasis in this area may give the world its genius, but often bestows the individual with internal pain.

When the planet Uranus came into humanity's consciousness, the individual, as a concept, became significant—the essence of the polarity became evident! When Uranus became apparent, the concept of morality for each individual was taken out of the realm of the local priest and put into a personal process. Liz Green says again that *"Uranus does say 'It shouldn't have to be like this,' ...Morality in the deepest sense comes from one's instinctive, heartfelt conviction of something not being in harmony with one's ideals, or what one perceives as the greatest good."* This personal awareness is most often a punishment, rather than a blessing. The ones who are singled out to pave the way to a New Order are often secured to a rock throughout the day—left to have their liver pecked out—to face the same process after a healing journey through the night.

History is peppered full of references to the Uranian person, whose individuality was sacrificed to the Greater Good of humanity. It is this person who is noted in history, because the average, ordinary person is not noteworthy. (And remember, the recognition for one's deeds is another trademark of the Fifth/ Eleventh's Polarity—the Fifth strives to obtain it, the Eleventh obtains it by merit of his strivings.) They bring revolution into every area of social development, from music to political change. The legend of the person is glorious, while the individual's personal life is often tragic..

If you follow the order that astrology follows —Fire creates, Earth materializes, Air conceptualizes, Water synthesizes—then you will find the essential meaning of the Eleventh Archetype. Melanie Reinhart said it quite succinctly when she said that it *"represents that process of soul growth which unfolds as we courageously debunk our own false godlikeness, discovering and giving up our inflations and identification with archetypal images."* If the creative archetype of this process is the search for meaning, then the Eleventh is the concept of what is ultimately meaningful.

Beyond the above, however, it clearly brings us into the conceptualization of the complete chart and its parts. In keeping with the Fourth Quadrant—a combination of the Objective Awareness of the Southern Hemisphere and the Awareness of Self of the Eastern Hemisphere—this Archetype is clearly an indication that we have the potential of acquiring an impetuous force that is seemingly from the beyond, while also allowing us to evaluate ourselves.

The Fifth strives to create the ideal Self through conscious awareness; the Eleventh conceptualizes the ideal world and shares that ideal with like-minded Others. In that spirit, the Eleventh's process is the integration of the individual with the cosmos. Truly, this archetype has the ability to lead us into our own particular level of the esoteric state… into whatever stratum of enlightenment we can personally absorb—hopefully without madness.

Chapter 20

The Twelfth Archetype

Neptune-Pisces-Twelfth House
Water - Mutable- Cadent

If Cancer synthesizes the course of action initiated by Aries, and Scorpio synthesizes the course of action initiated by Leo and Aries, then it follows that Pisces—the sign of the Twelfth—synthesizes the courses of action initiated by Sagittarius, Leo, and Aries... or, in other words, Pisces synthesizes the chart's complete course of action. It is like the color white: it possesses all the other colors.

To encapsulate, Cancer synthesizes primal development into the individual's subconscious mind. The subconscious constructs the womb of the conscious mind and forms the fertile embryonic condition that will give birth to the next course of action. Then, Scorpio refines "becoming conscious" into a spectrum of awareness and growth, which ultimately takes us into transformation. Scorpio's synthesis, which began in the dimness of the Second Quadrant, hurls us out of her dark, desolate waters into the search for life's meaning. This search is the genesis for the next, and final, course of action. The Twelfth is not only the synthesis of the last process, independently, but it synthesizes the entire Zodiacal process, because each Archetype is the transmutation of the last. This is paralleled by its polarity, the Sixth Archetype, which represents the transition Archetype from the Second Quadrant to the Third, from below the horizon to above it. In other words, Mutable Earth solidifies the processes that have preceded it, in preparation for encountering the 'other' above the horizon. Mutable Water represents the same process in the other direction. But here the surrender of self to a mystical, oceanic oneness precedes the coagulation of this oneness into a new self, and the cycle begins anew. To synthesize this final process, Pisces absorbs the entire development inside of her concavity and holds it as the Collective Unconscious—that theorized place of Carl Jung's where all things abide contemporaneously.

With this Twelfth Archetype, we've arrived at the end of the last Quartet of Elements. As we did with the Fourth and the Eighth—the synthesis of the Personal and the Social Quartet— let's now examine this synthesis in terms of this last Collective Quartet. As you read, begin thinking about what Cosmic Functions this foursome represents. Which structures in the Human Need hierarchy are represented? We could say Cognition, Ambition, Rebellion, and Dissolution. We might say Principle, Social Standing, Social Purpose, and Universal Love.

Structurally, the Twelfth is the end of the chart, but since everything is obviously cyclic, it is also the beginning. It's the place that many astrologers look to for information about Past Lives as well as other non-material information. I don't deny their insights; I just don't know how they can be certain of their findings. I'm very cautious about what I tell a client!

The truth is, however, whether it's past lives within this life, or past lives in the context of reincarnation, the statement is, on a higher level, the same. The Twelfth holds clues to the numinous past as it lives itself out in the present. Whether this is reincarnation, familial baggage, or the spiritual values that subtly influence our being, the nature of this archetype is that it's hidden and not directly accessible. The insights gleaned from this Twelfth Archetype form a perfect polarity with those gleaned from the Sixth. If the Sixth symbolizes issues of physical well-being, then the Twelfth symbolizes issues of spiritual well-being.

On the other hand, that part of the chart does hold a certain mystique. Let's take out some of the mystery by pondering the fact that astrology is a metaphoric language, spoken to us by the corporeal world. The astrological corporeal world includes our environment, our planet, but it goes beyond our immediate environment to include the entire solar system. (As a metaphor, I say, "Astrology takes us beyond Wal-Mart reality.")

Naturally, our planet is the central interpreter of this metaphoric language that the solar system introduces, just as we interpret what our environmental world introduces. Of course, this is a chicken-or-the-egg thing: does the corporeal world bring us the interpretations, or do we interpret the corporeal world for ourselves? This simple, popular question can find some sophisticated answers from the world of quantum physics.

In lecture at the *1994 Cycles & Symbols Conference*, the physicist William Keepin, Ph.D. referenced the work of David Bohm (a colleague of Einstein). Keepin was introducing his audience to the *"emerging fields of nonlinear dynamics and chaos theory, and in particular, fractal geometry."* When getting into the findings of David Bohm, he said that Bohm's deep quest for the essence of reality sent him to have extensive dialogues with spiritual masters, one of whom was the Indian mystic Krishnamurti.

He then took his audience through a systematic process, with the coup de grace being his explanation of Bohm postulating that the electron (a component of the atom) is a *"knowing structure"* (to paraphrase) within the atom, and in that structure, is carried the total information of the universe.

Keepin continued on explaining how Bohm had theorized that there's yet another level which exists that is a *"wave-like field."* This wave-like piece of information gives the electron access to the information about the rest of the physical universe. He called this *"the quantum potential, which is a wave-like information field that gives the electron access to information about the rest of the physical universe. Bohm was able to show that the influence of the quantum potential depended only on the form and not on the magnitude of this wave-form."*

Using David Bohm's theory for substantiation Dr. Keepin went on to say, that it's not that Pluto actually connects to one's brain. It's that the wave-form of Pluto is simultaneously going on in you. And Keepin said, *"Literally."*

This gives a clearer definition of astrology as a metaphoric language, based on the occurrences of physical phenomena. Since our physical world is made up of atoms, and the electron is the information-carrying component of the atom, then we are scientifically brought back to the holographic theory of our universe (any portion of a holographic image, no matter how small, carries the complete image).

It could also be said that Dr. Keepin gave a physicist's view of synchronicity. So, in considering the above, the Twelfth isn't just our past lives, but our future lives as well. It is metaphoric of the All Knowing within the Universe. It is the Alpha and the Omega—the true essence of God.

This area is the hardest to fully understand. It lays claim to the most imaginative, the most secretive, the most deceptive, the most sincere and holy, the most psychotic, the most personally debase and the most artistic. You find the Twelfth Archetype in every walk of life, in every type of situation. It truly is the pure essence of God—the all that is—and to look upon the face of God deems it complicated to live within what is known as reality.

When I was studying with Zipporah Dobyns, she gave us nine charts to take home for homework. She told us that some of the charts were from the data of holy men—gurus in India who were greatly respected for their beatification. The rest of the charts were those of winos, who were living on the street, begging for money to get their next cheap bottle of wine. We went home and worked into the wee hours; each of us thought that certainly we had, individually, distinguished between the two categories; but the next day, no one had arrived at the correct astrological answer. Dr. Dobyns astutely showed us that both the wino and the guru had the same chart with the same potential.

Let's take a moment to look at the physical position of the Twelfth House. It is located above the First House and above the Ascendant. Since the earth spins in a counter-clockwise motion, within a 24-hour period, the Sun and planets move around the earth in a clockwise motion. The chart—a representation of the earth—has the same planetary motion. Therefore, the traveling Sun will rise above the Ascendant and go into the Twelfth House. So, diurnal motion carries (metaphorically speaking) the rising Sun and the planets from the First House into the Twelfth House, then clockwise around the chart to set from the Seventh House into the Sixth House. Yet consider this: at the same time, annual motion carries the planets counterclockwise around the chart, from the Sixth into the Seventh, and from the Twelfth into the First. So, the process and symbology of this antagonistic action at the Ascendant has its polarity at the Descendant.

Everyone, at some time, has experienced a sunrise. There are two different, but distinct, physical manifestations at a sunrise: The first one is that suddenly there is a burst of dazzling, blinding light that pops up over the Horizon; the light is so intense, it's impossible to even look in the direction of the rising Sun. This was such a well-known fact that, when we engaged in wars where armies fought hand to hand, often the attacking army would move into position during the moonless night, so the defending faction would be facing the rising Sun. The next morning, as the attackers charged, the defenders would be "blinded by the light."

The second appearance of a sunrise is that the sunrise is totally covered by a dense mist or fog, and it takes until midmorning for it to burn off. In this case, the light is simply hidden. In this circumstance, as well as in the first, immediately after sunrise the physical area is nebulous and uncertain. In both situations, one's vision is obscured, and this is potentially dangerous. It is an area that can conceal secrets, such as secret enemies, whether this is a physical secret enemy or a psychological/psychic secret enemy.

One of the things that can be safely said about a person who exhibits the characteristics of a strong Twelfth Archetype is that they don't feel as if they fit into the mundane world. It's not a feeling of shyness like that which inundates her other Water sisters, but rather they feel as if they are in the correct place while the rest of the world isn't. They're usually quite arrogant about it, just matter of fact. My first formal astrology teacher said Pisces have one foot here and the other one over there, and they would just as soon be over there. She didn't say any more about it, and didn't need to. We all just knew what she meant. This ethereal, ephemeral quality of the Twelfth has its polarity in the Sixth, whose qualities represent a manifest pragmatism and an attention to mundane details. It's no surprise then that Mercury is both dignity and exalted in Virgo, while having its detriment in Pisces.

There is something innately melancholy about the Twelfth, whether it manifests with a strong placement of Neptune, with planets in the Twelfth House, or with a stellium in Pisces. They seem to be longing for something that is not quite known—something that is just out of their reach. There always seems to be the hope that the ultimate purpose of this life will come out of the darkness. There is the constant hope that some elevated consciousness—either as a human, or by some magic potion—will bring this profound mystery into the light.

In keeping with Liz Green's remarkable ability of putting pen to paper—or fingers to a key board—she brilliantly brought out this archetype in her book, *The Astrological Neptune and the Quest for Redemption.* In her introduction, she tweaks one's mind with questions, *"What...is this poignant yearning which justifies any sacrifice...? Is it truly the clear voice of the soul making itself heard through the prison walls of earthly substance? Or is it the desperate defense-mechanism of the fragile personality...How can we tell the difference, in our relentless search for messiahs and gurus..., between a Christ and a Hitler?"*

The powers of the Twelfth have always been considered a bit inauspicious to the normal world. This house rules hospitals, institutions, prisons, and specifically mental wards and mental hospitals. Therefore, by association (and as a good polarity to the Sixth Archetype) it rules the healers, including shamans, psychics, herbalists and the like—anything that has to do with connecting to the ethereal and bringing information back. And, even though the Eighth rules deep analysis, and the Seventh rules talk-therapy, the Twelfth rules those who walk the floors of the above-mentioned buildings—both the inmates and the folks who care for them.

The Twelfth, as the end result of everything that has transpired in the zodiacal development, will harvest an infinite possibility of human conditions. The products will be an array of victims and persecutors, the invalids and the caretakers, the insane and their keepers. In recent times it's medicine, rather than religion, which has stepped up to deal with this task.

Each of us has gone through the eleven separate development processes in one form or another, and at the end, we all come to the conclusion that the only potential place that is worthwhile to go, is back to the source—that oceanic utopia of non-existent bliss. This state is known as spirituality, or being in spirit form. It is a very inviting arena, and calls to us much like the sea nymphs called Sirens in Greek mythology, who, by their sweet singing, lured mariners to their destruction on the rocks. We all are drawn to this sweet music as we all look for the bliss of perfection.

The Latin word, *spiritus*, is the root word for spirit and spiritual. In the Roman culture, it was used simultaneously for the highest spiritual experience and for the vilest poison. And it doesn't matter if one has gone into a trance from meditating, or if one has smoked opium, the results are the same. The individual has been transported out of what is considered normal reality into an altered state of consciousness. Both bring a hallucinatory effect, and both take one into euphoria. It doesn't matter whether the experimenter is a wine maker, a shaman, or a chemist. If the truth was faced, all drugs are deadly poisonous. It's no accident that spirits is another word for alcoholic beverages. They both find rulership in this Twelfth Archetype.

In German, the word *Geist* translates both as spirit and as mental or mind. This can be understood further still in our English term mental illness, yet another area of Twelfth Archetype rulership. This isn't the mental-mind suggested by the Third Archetype, referring to conscious thought processes and verbal dexterity. But it can be like the mental processes of the Sixth where the focus of the mind narrows into obsessiveness. And their need to fix everything flows into neurosis. It refers, rather, to processes that still belong to an aspect of mind, having more to do with subtle influences residing there—influences of a more spiritual, etheric nature. And here we see, yet again, an interesting aspect of the nature of the Six –Twelve polarity, with both referring to what we may call mental disorders.

In the 1960s, when drugs became a prevalent focus in our culture, I came upon a supposition. I theorized that drugs actually kill a person to a degree proportionate to the power of the drug. For example, an aspirin wouldn't take one to a near-death experience; but opium would. Of course, any of it is dangerous, for even the aspirin is potentially a killer. We are drawn to this experience, however, because the high that one gets from this near-death experience is a temporary, but vicarious, closeness to the other side, and that's our attraction to the substance.

In ancient tribes, the shaman held the primary control over these substances. Today, however, they belong to a larger officialdom; the shaman has lost his importance. The spiritual has been removed in this medium and the new ruling god—Money— does not require sacredness in the ritual offerings (sacredness and rituals are another excellent Six-Twelve polarity). The ruling priests are clustered in the politics of the AMA and the Drug Lords. And the sacrifices they require are our old and our young. The AMA feeds on the old and the drug lords feed on our youth.

It's interesting that this is the Twelfth, right next door to the First, which is so survival-oriented. The drive to take drugs is a hypnotic, unconscious desire for the oceanic bliss from which we came, and our desire to come back—to cling to life as we know it—comes from our subconscious awareness that we've signed a pre-natal contract to do this lifetime. It has always been prevalent that some folks favor "going home," while others are more conscious of their connection to their "contract."

Most of us, though, go a little this way, and then run back the other way…with the respective ways corresponding to the health or addiction of the individual. This is because the reality we have manifested is too much to deal with constantly. In Reality, there is the constant reminder that we are separate, alone, and abandoned. Carl Jung expressed it well as he spoke about Roland H., saying, *"His craving for alcohol was the equivalent on a low level of the spiritual thirst of our being for wholeness, expressed in medieval language as, The union with God'…"*

Dr. J. Satinover, a Jungian analyst, pointed out in a 1987 lecture that what people look for in an "addictive experience" is normal. *"That is to say, the craving is normal…the craving for certain kinds of elation, for a certain sense of specialness, for heroism, for cessation of pain. Underlying all of them ultimately and most powerfully is the seeking for a sense of meaningfulness."* He then refers to Jung's recognition that the motivating factor here is that one is seeking spirit—the feeling of being one with the universe, or God.

Consequently a major focus of this Archetype is victimization. It seems that the more one can claim the role of victimhood, the more they feel they have a license to be addictive. Being addictive is not limited to drugs and alcohol. Some people are addicted to being ill, while others are addicted to television or to the movies; Neptune rules both of these. And then there are those who are simply addicted to being a victim.

The victim has had great popularity over the past two thousand or so years. One explanation is the fact that, astrologically, we have been living in the Piscean Age, which lasts about two thousand years (with a bit of an orb before and after). And what better way for the Piscean Age to be ushered in than with a martyred Messiah, who was not attached to the physical world, nor its paraphernalia, and who sacrificed himself for the good of all. Over this time-span, there have been thousands of souls, who have given their lives, either figuratively or literally, under the canopy of this ideal.

Liz Greene seems to agree with this, that these folks tend to *"enmesh themselves...in misfortune, illness and victimization in their emotional and physical lives..."* In her opinion (and it has been my observation, as well) that it's based on the belief that such will make them *"more pure and more acceptable in the eyes of that Other whom they seek..."* This conviction can separate the individual from his or her potential, while most likely manifesting an enormous shadowed persona. This can, and often does, spawn the need to lean toward alcohol or drugs to modify the torn identity.

On the other hand, and contrary to popular belief, a victim has a great deal of power. Those who are willing to give of themselves are busily connecting strings to the darkened corners of your life—those parts that live in the shadow. Guilt is the sticky substance out of which they make their web...that selfless, sacrificing mother, or the helping neighbor, or the friend, who is so willing to give you so much, then tells you how to live your life. You can't possibly be rude to them, after all they've done so much for you! Yet, you are feeling manipulated, and again, you feel guilty because you are feeling manipulated.

When one is being manipulated, he is under the control of the manipulator. It is clear that the victim holds the ultimate power. If the power shifts, then they can go out into the world and show their wounds, and you become the persecutor. However, this victim number is important to grasp as a low-octave, dysfunctional expression of the Twelfth Archetype's dynamic. It comes up as a very Piscean yearning to truly help others–to surrender ego desires and offer them up to something greater. This is best grasped as an elegant polarity to the Sixth Archetype's dynamic of service.

The artist is yet another expression of the Twelfth—from music that can transport us onto an altered dimension, to the colors and lines that can speak to us from a canvas, to the special effect artist who can carry us through nebulous film into a the ecstasy of make-believe.

However, this threshold is delicate and can lead to insanity or genius…Whichever prevails, the artist can truly elevate our common minds into a greater awareness. We not only tolerate the artist's insanity and call it idiosyncratic, but many times we glamorize the life and view it as romantic. Many aspire to emulate the artist's lifestyle— often they are society's heroes. Those living in their personal torment are amazed at this response. They feel their lives are made up of mirrors: that they are walking through a life of illusion. But they and the others living with this knowledge have a greater under-standing than those who think all of this is real. Who truly knows what part is real and what part is illusion? Robert Hand expressed this well in a lecture I heard in San Francisco in 1988, when he said, *"Saturn is the illusion there's a reality; Neptune is the proof there's not!"*

Donna Cunningham has voiced a goodly account of "Neptunians" on a number of occasions that I've either read or witnessed in lecture. What we consider reality, she called "Assumed Reality". She explained that she called it that because most of us assume that what we experience is all there really is and we assume, as well, that this reality is the same for everyone. But in actuality, Assumed Reality is *"a flexible, fluid medium, not the same for any two individuals or for the same individual at any two points in time."* She brings to mind different viewpoints of individuals witnessing the same experience, based on their immediate mindset…whether one is ill and another is intimidated, while a third has just started a new relationship and the whole world looks rosy.

Actually, with the idea that "reality is in the eyes of the Beholder," we have come full circle. It all goes off into a foggy infinity as to what's real and what's not real. And in the earlier chapter, Introducing the Archetypes, it was scientifically postulated that "Everything is Everything." Of course, every Sunday School child knows that God is Everything…the Alpha and the Omega! But, if "Everything" is real, then nothing is. We are left with a huge "Everything" that only has subjective definition. What, however, are we left with?

Liz Greene said in a lecture presented at the 1985 Neptune Conference in San Francisco that to understand Neptune, she went to the Kabala. She said that the planet *"seems to be connected with Kater and it means crown. What this symbolizes is that it's the big toe of God; it's as high as we can reach to the ineffable ..."* She explains that *beyond that point there is "no thing"; it is the very top of the "Tree of Life."* At that point – the Kater – we can get *"some kind of 'glimpse'. That glimpse is what we call 'God.'"*

According to Ms. Greene's reference, we can only hope to achieve a "Big Toe" concept of God. We can never hope to see more of the Most Supreme, and we can only see the Big Toe part under suitable conditions. Moreover, many who have an experience with the Big Toe could not tolerate it and are now considered insane. Others simply suffer—either from the longing for the connection, or from the lack of longing.

True spirituality is the ability to be in complete harmony with the Universe. The closest religious belief to this is Zen Buddhism, and in that religion, there is no god-head. One simply follows their breath and honors other life, the moment, and completely focuses on their immediate activity. Zen practitioners claim that their road to enlightenment is not in opposition to any religious belief...that a belief system and their discipline are not even in the same category. Considering that the Ninth is at a difficult angle to the Twelfth, they could be correct in that assessment.

The Twelfth Archetype—Fourth Quadrant, Yin, Mutable, Water—is placed at a polarity to Sixth Archetype—Second Quadrant, Yin, Mutable, Earth. The essence of the Twelfth Archetype can be said to be Surrender. There is little of the Twelfth that cannot be under-stood in this context. It's interesting to consider Mutable Earth as a polarity to this, with its penchant for organization, discreet placement, ritual and fastidiousness, finding completion in surrendering that up to a sense of the oceanic. The spirituality implied by the Twelfth Archetype and the spirituality implied by the Sixth Archetype is interesting to consider in light of the quadrants. The Fourth Quadrant suggests an objective view of self, while the Second suggests a subjective view of Other. Ironic to think that a truly objective view of self occurs in this last phase by a surrender and a dissolution of the self. This is the stuff of enlightenment. Don't expect to begin to grasp it with the rational mind alone. After all, Mercury is in both Fall and Detriment here.

Chapter 21

The End—
Or Is It the Beginning?

Even though there are many fields of knowledge that are encompassed in a thorough examination of astrology, the study you have just completed will take you into the essence of counseling astrology. It takes you into motivations and behavior, and now that you have finished your inquisition of the twelve Archetypes, it should be obvious that planets, signs and houses are more than just simply astrological components. It should also be evident that each represents a basic drive within the human psyche—a drive that motivates the behavior, on some level, of every individual around the world. Each of the Archetypes is buried deep within a person—whether that person knows astrology or not. Moreover, each drive, or Archetype, encompasses a wide range of expressions.

An Archetype is a model, so it's interesting to see how each culture creates its own models, which then form and shape its society. Even though each has a different way of expressing the needs and responses of the culture, each has a Venus, or an Aphrodite... a Mars, or an Ares. Every culture holds images of duty and responsibility, or optimism and expansion. But upon examination, each of the endless variations of a given myth can fit into a subcategory of the twelve basic Archetypes. Since each of the twelve represents an intrinsic drive or response, these twelve can be considered a grouping that holds the key to the fundamentals of human behavior.

The Archetypes, however, don't simply affect individuals. Whole generations are imprinted with particular archetypal combinations. In addition, one of my favorite pastimes through the years has been to ascertain accurate birth data for a cat or dog, then to observe the animal's day-to-day behavior. You can't pre-program an animal to respond to a planet or sign; they act out their specific combination of archetypal behavior perfectly and purely.

My hope has always been that this material will help students learn not only to speak the language of astrology, but that it will take them to a place in which the Archetypes speak to them—whether the "words" are truly spoken or simply seen in one's actions, choices, and daily life.

Combining the Archetypes offers so many variables that only an in-depth understanding of the subject—an understanding that goes far beyond mere intellectual knowledge—will allow one to integrate the multiplicity of factors involved. For example, if you multiply the planets, Chiron and the four asteroid goddesses by the twelve Zodiacal signs, and then multiply that by the possible house placements, you end up with 2,160 possibilities. It's no wonder that readers of the popular Sun-sign columns in newspapers around the world don't grasp the depth and breadth of insight that a comprehensive knowledge of astrology and the Archetypes offers.

Individuals who do choose to undertake a more intensive study of astrology go far beyond anything that keyword memorization offers and soon learn that this is an unending study. Just when you think you've reached the "end" of a particular subject—and that there's nothing new to learn—the circle turns, and you're back at the beginning once again. For the Zodiac itself is a circle, and the beginning and end cannot be separated.

Learning astrology goes beyond mere study, however, becoming for most a passion and a part of one's daily life. Astrology is not a religion, in my opinion, but it can give one a road to spirituality, if that's what is desired. It is not a hard science, but there are some areas within the astrological framework that are quite scientific. It's not a philosophy, but many find themselves drawn to this area of study as a natural adjunct to their astrological work.

Perhaps, when all is said and done, astrology is composed of something of each of these—a belief, a passion, a philosophy of life, a science of sorts, a tool for daily living, a way to learn about yourself and your motivations, and a guide along the sometimes difficult road of life. It's not the definition of the word astrology that is of consequence, however. Like-wise, pinpointing the "why"—determining the underlying reason that prompted you to begin a serious study of the subject—isn't necessary. What is truly important is to enjoy the journey!

Endnotes

Chapter 1:

Tarnas, Richard, PhD. *Cycles & Symbols Conference*, San Francisco, 1990.

Ibid

Chapter 2:

Dobyns, Zipporah. In a class lecture, Houston, Texas, 1982 *Paulus Alexandrinus, Introductory Matters,* translated by Robert Schmidt, Project Hindsight, Greek Track, Volume 1, pgs. vii-viii, The Golden Hind Press, 1993

Chapter 3:

Elwell, Dennis. *Cycles & Symbols Conference*, San Francisco, 1990.

Campbell, Joseph. *The Hero With A Thousand Faces.* Second Edition. United States, Princeton University Press, page 6

Green, Liz. *The Astrology of Fate.* First Edition. United States, Samuel Weiser, Inc., 1983, page 166.

Chapter 4:

Taylor, Thomas (1758–1835), translation. "Orphic Hymn 65 to Ares" from Wikipedia, the free encyclopedia, Public Domain

Favonian. *Ares.* Wikipedia, edited 25 October 2011.

Burkert, Walter. *Greek Religion.* Malden, MA, English translations Blackwell Publishing, Ltd. & Harvard University Press 1985. page 169

Green, Liz. *The Astrology of Fate.* First Edition. United States, Samuel Weiser, Inc., 1983, page 73.

Chapter 4, continued:
Green, Liz. *The Astrology of Fate*. First Edition. United States, Samuel Weiser, Inc., 1983, page 81.

ibid.

ibid.

Chapter 5:
Evelyn-White, Hugh G. translated. "Homeric Hymn to Aphrodite," Hesiod, the Homeric hymns, and Homerica,.

London, W. Heinemann; New York, The Macmillian Company, 1914, from Wikipedia, Public Domain.

Bible. New Testament, King James version. I Corinthian 7:9.

Chapter 6:
Evelyn-White, Hugh G. translated. "Homeric Hymn to Hermes," Hesiod, the Homeric hymns, and Homerica,. London, W. Heinemann; New York, The Macmillian Company, 1914, from Wikipedia, the free encyclopedia, Public Domain.
Collier's Encyclopedia. Volume 17. New York: Collier's 1972, page 590

Green, Liz. *The Astrology of Fate*. First Edition. United States, Samuel Weiser, Inc., 1983, pgs 190 & 192,

Thurman, Michael. "Astrology and the New Physics". *The Mountain Astrologer,* February/March 1996.

Collier's Encyclopedia, 1986 Edition.

Keepin, William, PhD. Cycles & Symbols Conference, San Francisco, 1995.

Chapter 7:
Campbell, Joseph. *The Masks of God: Occidental Mythology.* Sixth Edition. United States, Penguin Books, 1976, pg 7

Lao Tzu, Arthur Waley translator. *The Way and Its Power: Kai Tzu's Tao Te Ching and Its Place in Chinese Thought.* New York: Grove Press, 1958.

Guralnik, David B., Dictionary Editor in Chief. *Webster's New World Dictionary of the American Language.* Concise Edition. Nashville, TN: The Southwestern Company, 1972

Campbell, Joseph. *The Masks of God: Occidental Mythology.* Sixth Edition. United States, Penguin Books, 1976, page 17
Ibid, page 18

von Goethe, Johann Wolfgang, Edward Dowden, translation. *West-östlicher Diwan.*

Chapter 8:
Neumann, Erich, R. F. C. Hull, translation. *The Origins and History of Consciousness.* First Princeton/Bollingen Paperback Printing, 1970, page 40

ibid, pg. 45

ibid, pg. 89

Chapter 9:
Hand, Robert. *Horoscope Symbols.* First Edition. Gloucester, MA, Para Research, Inc., pg. 223.

Chapter 10:
Hay, Louise. *You Can Heal Your Life.* First Edition. Carlsbad, CA. Hay House Publishing, 1984, pg. 127.

Chapter 11:
Evelyn-White, Hugh G. translated. "Homeric Hymn to Demeter," Hesiod, the Homeric hymns, and Homerica,. London, W. Heinemann; New York, The Macmillian Company, 1914,

from Wikipedia, the free encyclopedia, Public Domain.
Jung, Carl G. and Karl Kerenyi. *Essays on a Science of Mythology.* Harper & Row, 1963, pg. 148.

Chapter 12:
George, Demetra with Douglas Bloch. *Asteroid Goddesses, The Mythology, Psychology and Astrology of the Reemerging Feminine.* First Edition. ACS Publications, Inc., 1986, pg. 117 ibid. pg. 118

Chapter 14:
Evelyn-White, Hugh G. translated. "Homeric Hymn to Pallas Athena," Hesiod, the Homeric hymns, and Homerica,. London, W. Heinemann; New York, The Macmillian Company, 1914,

from Wikipedia, the free encyclopedia, Public Domain.

Greene, Liz. *Astrology for Lovers.* Second Edition. United States, Samuel Weiser, Inc., 1989, page 13.

Chapter 15:
Evelyn-White, Hugh G. translated. "Homeric Hymn to Hera," Hesiod, the Homeric hymns, and Homerica,. London, W. Heinemann; New York, The Macmillian Company, 1914, from Wikipedia, the free encyclopedia, Public Domain.

Fellini, Fedreico, Isabel Quigley, translation. *Fellini on Fellini.* New York, Delacorte Press/S. Lawrence, 1976. pg. 83

Chapter 16:
MacMillion Dictionary of Psychology. Senior Edition, 1989

Jung, Carl G., Gerhard Adler and R.F.C. Hull, Translation. *Two Essays on Analytical Psychology (Collected Works of C.G. Jung, Volume 7).* Revised 2nd edition, Bollingen Series, Princeton, NJ: Princeton University Press, 1966, pg 78.

Campbell, Joseph. *The Masks of God: Occidental Mythology.* Sixth Edition. United States, Penguin Books, 1976, pg. 49

Green, Liz. *The Astrology of Fate.* First Edition. United States, Samuel Weiser, Inc., 1983, pg. 39
ibid

Chapter 16, continued:
Jung, Carl G. Tavistock Lectures on "Analytical Psychology".
London, 1935.

ibid.

ibid.

ibid.

Green, Liz. *The Astrology of Fate.* First Edition. United States,
Samuel Weiser, Inc., 1983, pgs. 49 & 50

Hillman, James. *The Dream and the Underworld.* New York,
Harper & Row, Publishers, Inc.1979, pg. 27.

Williams, Carlos William. *Spring and All.* "The Ivory Crown".
Robert McAlmon Contact Publishing Company, 1923.

Green, Liz. *The Astrology of Fate.* First Edition. United States,
Samuel Weiser, Inc., 1983, pg. 65

Chapter 17:
Campbell, Joseph. *The Masks of God: Occidental Mythology.*
Sixth Edition. United States, Penguin Books, 1976, Pg. 21
ibid., pg. 148

Chapter 18:
Green, Liz. *The Astrology of Fate.* First Edition. United States,
Samuel Weiser, Inc., 1983, pg. 209

Green, Liz. *Saturn: A New Look at an Old Devil.* First Edition.
York Beach, ME, Samuel Weiser, Inc. 1976 pg. 10,
ibid., pg. 11

Green, Liz. *The Astrology of Fate.* First Edition. United States,
Samuel Weiser, Inc., 1983, pg. 243
Green, Liz. *Saturn: A New Look at an Old Devil.* First Edition.
York Beach, ME, Samuel Weiser, Inc. 1976 pg. 10,

ibid.

ibid.

Chapter 18, continued:
Dobyn, Zipporah, Ph.D. *The Book of Saturn.* United States, ACS Publications, 1997, pg. 107

Chapter 19:
Green, Liz. *The Astrology of Fate.* First Edition. United States, Samuel Weiser, Inc., 1983, pg. 251

Tarnas, Richard. *Prometheus the Awakener.* First Edition. Oxford. Auriel Press, Ltd. 1993, pg. 10

ibid, pg. 11

ibid.

Aeschylus (assumed author), E. H. Plumptre, translation. *Prometheus Bound,* The Harvard classics. New York. P.F. Collier & Son 1914, Volume VIII, Part 4.

One of the primary things I've become aware of with this 5th/11th polarity is that there is no place where egos run amuck quite as much as within an organization. It is my opinion that because organizations and groups are usually made up of people who are working for a cause, and usually for little or no monetary compensation, their fulfillment is the reflection they get back for their efforts. This demonstrates the polarity excellently. Nonetheless, both are interested in individualism, but one is below the horizon and more interested in its subjective development of self-awareness, while the other is above the horizon and more interested in its objective development into the world.

The Fifth House is "playing," such as pleasure, relaxation, and performances. The Eleventh is groups, cliques, and popularity, which are types of playing as well. Financial Astrologers use the Eleventh as the corporation's money, and it is common knowledge that one looks to the Fifth when one wants to go gambling, which includes buying stocks.

Also, see the metaphor of "sun" here, as another connection with the polarity. In this regard, the Sun also relates to consciousness…to becoming aware.

Chapter 19 continued:
Green, Liz. *The Art of Stealing Fire, Uranus in the Horoscope.*
London. Centre for Psychological Astrology Press, BCM, 1996,
pg. 7

ibid. pg. 1

ibid. pg. 8

Reinhart, Melanie. *Chiron and the Healing Journey: An
Astrological and Psychological Perspective.* First Edition.
London, England, Penguin Group, 1989, pg. 30

ibid.

ibid.

Green, Liz. *The Art of Stealing Fire, Uranus in the Horoscope.*
London. Centre for Psychological Astrology Press, BCM, 1996,
pg. 18

Reinhart, Melanie. *Chiron and the Healing Journey: An
Astrological and Psychological Perspective.* First Edition.
London, England, Penguin Group, 1989, pg. 30

Chapter 20:
Keepin, William. *Cycles & Symbols Conference.* San Francisco,
CA. 1994. A complete transcript of this lecture can be found in
the August/September 1995 issue of *The Mountain Astrologer.*
Keepin, William. *Cycles & Symbols Conference.* San Francisco,
CA. 1994.

ibid.

Greene, Liz. *The Astrological Neptune and the Quest for
Redemption.* First Edition. Samuel Weiser, York Beach, ME,
1996, pg xiii

Jung, Carl G. Letter to William G. Wilson, Alcoholics
Anonymous, Box 459 Grand Central Station, New York 17, N.Y.
January 30, 1961

Satinover, Jeffrey, MS, MD, Fellow in Psychiatry and Child
Psychatry at Yale University and past president of the C. G. Jung
Foundation. Recorded lecture, 1987.

Chapter 20, continued:

Greene, Liz. *The Astrological Neptune and the Quest for Redemption.* First Edition. Samuel Weiser, York Beach, ME, 1996, pg xviii

ibid.

Hand, Robert. *Toward a Theory of Divination.* I.S.I.S. Workshop, San Francisco, 1988

Cunningham, Donna. Internationally respected astrologer with 35+ years of experience and thousands of articles on metaphysical topics.

Greene, Liz. "Neptune and the Therapeutic Process". Lecture presented at the Neptune Conference, San Francisco, CA 1985

ibid.

ibid.

About the Illlustrations:

A few of the illustrations in this book are computer graphics or hand drawings by Maria Kay Simms. These include the mandala designs used on a few chapter title pages, the chart wheels, the moons (pg. 54), Venus on page 88 (with apologies to Botticelli), and the phoenix (pg.102). Otherwise, Maria adapted the majority of the classic drawings of gods and goddesses, using Photoshop software, from public domain line art based on engravings of ancient Greek and Roman statuary, as shown in the book, *The Complete Encyclopedia of Illustration* by J.G. Heck, Park Lane, New York, a division of Crown Publications, Inc. In just a few cases, for deities not shown in the illustration book, she adapted art found by online search for "public domain art: Greek or Roman deities." The decorative astrology glyphs are from the font, "Ann's Astro," purchased from *www.fonts.com.*

About the Author

Ena Stanley has been nominated three times for the Regulus Award in Education. and was the first person to receive NCGR's Level IV Certification in the field of education. She started her personal study of astrology in 1968 and started her formal study in the late 1970's with Beverly Farrell, PMAFA. Her education went on through the first half of the 1980's with several noted astrologers, including intense studies with, Zipporah Dobyns and Joan Negus.

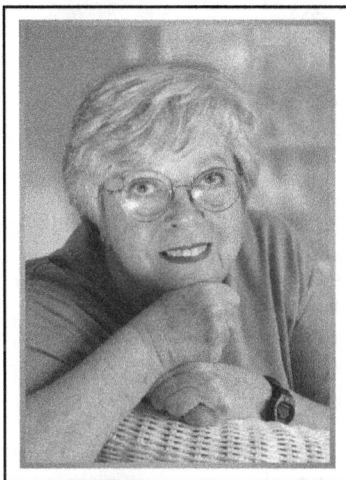

In January of 1986, Ena began her career as a teacher and built a curriculum to accommodate certification programs. She taught at Southern Oregon State College, 1986-1989; College of the Mainland (Galveston County, Texas), 1990-1993; Gulf Coast Chapter NCGR, 1994-1995 and CALCampus, an exclusively on-line community college, January 1995—Spring, 1997.

In July of 1997, Ena and Ed Perrone created and opened the first cyberspatial astrological school through an experimental contract with NCGR; but upon realizing the broad potential of this medium, they decided not to remain exclusive. Subsequently Online College of Astrology was born.

By 2008, the term "online" was no longer unique, so a contest was organized to select a newer and more appropriate name for the school. The International Academy of Astrology was decided upon. IAA is a vocational school, dedicated to offering the serious astrology student a wide-ranging and comprehensive education. Many distinguished astrologers have contributed to its curriculum and it is respected in the astrological community for its multiplicity—no one particular model or belief is the focus, giving each student the tools to explore any number of factions.

Ena claims to be IAA's "gate keeper." This translates into a devotion to the daily duties that keep IAA running smoothly.

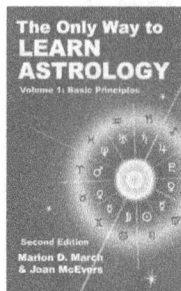
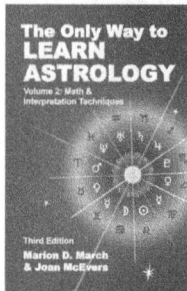

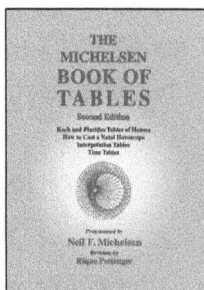

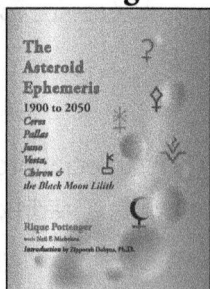

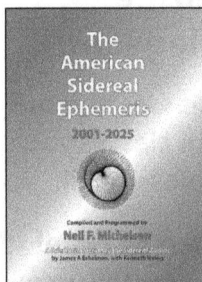

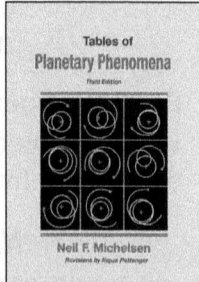